Praise for *In Suppo*

T0247934

"Katie and Kristan do a wonderful job p̶r̶.̶.̶.̶.̶.̶.̶.̶g̶ ̶.̶.̶.̶.̶.̶.̶.̶.̶.̶.̶ ̶.̶.̶.̶.̶.̶.̶ ̶.̶.̶.̶.̶.̶ strategies, action plans, and ingredients for a MTSS of teaching and learning. They provide the reader with ongoing personal anecdotes, analogies, and steps of MTSS and many opportunities throughout to pause, think, and reflect on how to best support all students. The book highlights how all learners are 'capable of greatness' with the appropriate shift in systems and priorities."

—**Michael W. Adams**, *EdD, Executive Director,*
American Schools of Central America,
Colombia-Caribbean and Mexico (Tri-Association)

"As an educator of 30 years and currently serving as MTSS Coordinator, I believe *In Support of Students* is empowering! Whether you are an educator in the first stage of implementing MTSS or already full-steam ahead, this book provides a blueprint that is proactive and responsive to student success for all learners. The authors take you on a journey through change, crafting a vision, planning for success, and action steps to an inclusive multi-tiered system of supports. Reflection questions posed throughout the book are a bonus to provoke conversation for the reader and district teams. This is the real deal for educators looking to create and sustain an equitable MTSS!"

—**Lorri Race**, *MTSS Coordinator 6–12,*
Norwich City School District

"Intentionally designing our educational systems to ensure inclusive experiences rooted in belonging for all students is not the work for leaders faint of heart. In *In Support of All Students: A Leader's Guide to Equitable MTSS*, authors Katie Novak and Kristan Rodriguez have integrated their vast knowledge of universal design for learning (UDL) and implementation/improvement science to assist equity warriors in their journey of self-reflection, organizational improvement, and ultimately creating a system that benefits those we serve. A must-read and call to action."

—**Kevin Schaefer**, *Director, Inclusive Practices,*
Supporting Inclusive Practices (SIP) Project,
El Dorado County Office of Education

"Dr. Katie Novak and Dr. Kristan Rodriguez deliver again! School and district leaders and MTSS teams will benefit from this practical how-to guide that walks readers through the development/refinement of a school's multi-tiered system of support through the lens of UDL. The authors share practical tips, tools, and tales that can be used by teams to deepen their knowledge of MTSS and improve their systems so that every student can thrive."

—**Molly McCabe**, *Instructional Services,*
Riverside County Office of Education

"In *In Support of Students: A Leader's Guide to Equitable MTSS*, Dr. Novak and Dr. Rodriguez provide a clear, concise pathway to the change needed in our schools to support all students. They have demystified equitable MTSS implementation, providing the connections between what we talk about doing and the steps we can take to do it, placing students at the center— guiding the process of adapting our school environments into places where all students are included and learn!"

—**Annie Lamberto**, *Special Education and Inclusionary Practices,*
Washington Education Association

"This book is an excellent playbook for any school administrator to follow to get equitable MTSS going in their district. Whether this is your introduction to MTSS or you are well on your way, this book is the reference that you need to make the transformative changes in your school in order to truly support all students."

—**Steven C. Meyer**, *Superintendent,*
Clinton Public Schools

"This book is a must-read for any leader looking to make their school or district meet the increasingly diverse needs of all students. Written by practitioners for practitioners, it is a roadmap to follow, including many opportunities for collaboration and reflection built into each chapter."

—**Dr. Matthew Crowley**, *Superintendent,*
Woburn Public Schools

"*In Support of Students* stands out among other books that are focused on MTSS in that Novak and Rodriguez focus on change and improvement science strategies to incorporate a comprehensive and equitable multi-tiered system of support. As always, Katie and Kristan incorporate their sense of humor and relatable anecdotes to make sense of complex changes like this."

—**Henry J. Turner**, *EdD, Award-Winning High School Principal and Author of* Change the Narrative: How to Foster an Antiracist Culture in Your School

"Katie Novak and Kristan Rodriguez have delivered a truly empowering gift. *In Support of Students: A Leader's Guide to Equitable MTSS* is a how-to guide that delivers not only the tools and resources for learning leaders, but the strategies and models to examine current systems to support implementation of an authentic tiered system of support. Now we can finally answer the question 'Where do I start?' Through their candid storytelling and reflections at the onset of each chapter, Katie and Kristan connect with readers at such a genuine personal and professional level. Get ready to be equipped to lead inclusive, equitable, and sustainable change!"

—**Jennifer Knight DeLashmutt**, *Director of Curriculum and Professional Learning, International School Bangkok*

"Katie Novak and Kristan Rodriguez have written a must-read guide for systems to move beyond theory and planning to actionable systemic changes for all of our children to be successful and engaged in their learning. This book is invaluable for all levels of educational leaders."

—**Krestin Bahr**, *Superintendent, Peninsula School District*

"Every student deserves the very best education. Katie Novak and Kristan Rodriguez advocate for all students by coaching school leaders to design school and classroom systems that support every child's access to the grade-level curriculum. This is a book for school leaders and leadership teams looking to break free from the 'that's how we've always done it' mindset and entertain ideas and change that will support learners' academic, behavioral, and social needs. The 'Pause and Reflect' questions used in this book are a lifeline for school leaders looking to change their mindsets and systems."

—**Joanna Shelley**, *Educator*

In Support of Students

In Support of Students

A Leader's Guide to Equitable MTSS

Katie Novak, Ed.D.
Kristan Rodriguez, Ph.D.

JB JOSSEY-BASS™

A Wiley Brand

Published by Jossey-Bass
A Wiley Brand
111 River St., Hoboken NJ 07030
www.josseybass.com

Printed in the United States of America
Published simultaneously in Canada

Jossey-Bass books and products are available through most bookstores. To contact Jossey-Bass directly call our
Customer Care Department within the U.S. at 800-956-7739, outside the U.S. at 317-572-3986, or fax 317-572-4002.

Wiley publishes in a variety of print and electronic formats and by print-on-demand. Some
material included with standard print versions of this book may not be included in e-books or in print-on-
demand.

If this book refers to media such as a CD or DVD that is not included in the version you purchased, you may
download this material at http://booksupport.wiley.com.

For more information about Wiley products, visit www.wiley.com.

Library of Congress Cataloging-in-Publication Data

Names: Novak, Katie, author. | Rodriguez, Kristan, author. | Jossey-Bass Inc., publisher.
Title: In support of students : a leader's guide to equitable MTSS / Katie Novak, Kristan Rodriguez.
Description: San Francisco : Jossey-Bass, [2023] | Includes bibliographical references and index.
Identifiers: LCCN 2022059970 (print) | LCCN 2022059971 (ebook) | ISBN   9781119885269 (paperback) |
   ISBN 9781119885283 (adobe pdf) | ISBN   9781119885276 (epub)
Subjects: LCSH: Multi-tiered systems of support (Education). | Educational equalization. | Students--Services for.
Classification: LCC LB1029.M85 N68 2023 (print) | LCC LB1029.M85 (ebook) | DDC 379.2/6--dc23/
   eng/20221219
LC record available at https://lccn.loc.gov/2022059970
LC ebook record available at https://lccn.loc.gov/2022059971

Cover Design: Wiley
Cover Image: Trees: © discan/Getty Images Paper Texture: © xamtiw/Getty Images

SKY10051018_071123

This book is for educational leaders who believe that we can create more inclusive and equitable systems, that change is possible, and that our learners, especially those who have been excluded, minoritized, marginalized, and have had to be resilient, deserve so much more.

Contents

Acknowledgments

From Katie

To KRod, you paved my road to leadership, and for that, I am forever grateful. You saw leadership capacity in me before anyone else, and your perseverance (and the fact that you never take no for an answer! Ha!) encouraged me to expand my classroom walls further and further. From our first meeting in Chelmsford to the many years we collaborated in G-D (Dream Team!) to our ongoing work around the world, you will always be my BPF (Best Professional Friend). Can't wait to celebrate this book in PR. I'm coming! Love you so much.

To our team at Wiley, especially Natalie Muñoz, Mary Beth Rosswurm, and Christine O'Connor, your organization and support have been so helpful throughout this process. I am prone to biting off a bit more than I can chew, but your timeline, your reminders, and your check-ins kept us on track on this one. Kim Wimpsett and Amy Handy, we are so grateful for your eagle eyes during the editing process. I am grateful for the opportunity to share our work on a larger scale with leaders worldwide. Truly, I am humbled.

To my colleagues at Novak Education and the many partners and clients I work with, you continue to inspire me, push me, and teach me. Without your feedback, support, love, and laughs, this work wouldn't be as rewarding. To Lindie and Ashley especially, thank you for always helping me to keep it real.

And to my amazing family:

Lon, if I could go back, I would choose you all over again. Thank you for stepping away from your work to support mine. You are the best husband, dad, and partner in crime (although you aren't nearly as funny as me!). Truly, none of this would be possible without you. To Torin, Aylin, Brec, and Boden, this work is driven by my love for each of you. You deserve classrooms that accept you for who you are and provide you with the conditions you need to be wildly successful. Every parent wants that for their children and they shouldn't have to work so hard to get it. When systems work seems overwhelming, I think of you. I always say that every child is somebody's baby, and they deserve the very best. You are my babies and you make me better and happier every day. I am so proud of the people you are.

From Kristan

There is literally only one person who fits into my size fours and sixes as maternity wear, vigorously drinks decaffeinated coffee by the gallon, and whose opinion I intrinsically know is aligned with my vision, values, and goals as an educator, friend, and business partner. The Katie Novak is a blessing I have been given in this lifetime. I am forever grateful for the years we saw each other every day and missing you like crazy on this island.

To my partner in life, Rafael, for being my strength, my love, and my biggest supporter. You are simply and magically my everything. To my children, Rafael, Xavier, and Gabriel, you have grown into talented and visionary men. I am humbled by what you have done with your gifts. To my parents, Dan and Diane, who have always been my mentors, and my sister, Samantha, who was always my second mother, I love you all and am appreciative for the journey you took with me these many years.

To the amazing group of professionals I get to work with every day at Commonwealth Consulting Agency, I am left speechless by your dedication (and that is saying something). To our clients for whom we offer our hearts and minds, we value our relationships with you and our only success is realized through yours. May the future of every child continue to be the spark that lights us all. To my crazy crew of entrepreneurs in Palmas, who invite me daily to converse and learn and grow together, you are the new fountain from which I drink. Lastly, to the amazing team at Wiley, who have kept us on track, on word count, and with task and purpose in mind, I am thankful beyond measure.

Introduction

Recently, while scrolling through social media, an advertisement for a shirt stood out. It noted, "If you're not angry, you're not paying attention." In education, we know the outcomes of our learners and we know we can do better. Teachers are working way too hard not to have a greater impact on the outcomes of all students, especially those learners who have been historically underserved. Educators around the country are burnt out, over-worked, and overwhelmed. These realities are maddening. Despite this, we believe at our core that all students and all educators can experience success when schools and systems get the conditions right for them to be successful. And this requires a systems overhaul. A big one.

Federal education law requires the adoption of multi-tiered systems of support to ensure that every student has equitable access to grade-level classrooms, equitable opportunities to learn at high levels, and equitable feelings of belonging and hope. Numerous texts offer theories and concep-tual frames for creating these systems, but don't offer the tools to actually put them into practice. We both understand conceptually how ships sail and love the idea of a cruise down to the island of Nevis but we sure as heck don't know how to build a yacht. Understanding a theory and understand-ing how to put that theory into practice are not the same. Any attempts to build a boat without concrete tools would result in the edu-version of *Gilligan's Island* (note: lost at sea).

Similarly, leaders and school boards love the idea of inclusive and equi-table systems and are committed to the mission of meeting the needs of all learners. What is missing is the guidance on how to accomplish this. We have to provide tools and guidance so that people know how to build the ship, and more importantly, can sail it on both calm waters and choppy seas.

As the authors of this text, we are in a unique position as practitioners, lead authors of state MTSS guidance, and consultants with hundreds of districts worldwide to support district and school leaders in creating inclusive, equitable systems using a conversational style, concrete planning tools, numerous analogies, and just the right amount of sass. Thank you for joining us.

1

Planning for Systems Change

In this chapter, we introduce multi-tiered systems through the lens of complex change theory. Creating robust MTSS requires adaptive change throughout organizations. Facilitating this level of change requires an understanding of complex change, implementation science, and improvement science as drivers of success. We offer a Deeper Learning Model for MTSS, which explicitly connects MTSS to critical equity work and highlights the importance of deep, authentic learning experiences for all students.

The View from My Window (Kristan)

Recently, I moved to the eastern coast of Puerto Rico. Each night, I fall asleep to two sounds—the call of the coqui frog and the "woosh" of breaking waves. As the sun peeks out in the morning, the waves serve as an ancient siren song, luring me into the ocean. However, I have yet to heed that call. Instead, I sit at my desk, my fingers on the keyboard, staring at the blue light until I'm too exhausted to consider a moonlight voyage. It seems obvious that I should slam the laptop shut, walk over to the marina I can see from my terrace, and sail away. I promise that someday soon, I will charter a catamaran to Culebra, an island that encompasses wonders beneath its waves, spending a day filled with white sand, calm waters, and the sea life that I only see in the framed photos on my office wall.

It is not like I haven't taken some steps toward this goal. I even bought a snorkel! It currently sits in a drawer, in its plastic packaging, not yet having had the chance to peek at the leatherback turtles that hatch off my island shore that serves as protected land. I have the desire, the equipment, and the vision. But I have not yet taken all the steps necessary to change. It's time.

Our Call

We have all been engulfed by waves of educational shifts that pull us to make changes. While the past few years have taught us resiliency, they have also taught us that what we thought was, and always would be, the model for education in this country is quite malleable. If ever there was a time for us to evaluate our systems to design ones that can be more proactive, more responsive, and more successful, it is now.

Like us, you know, without a doubt, that educators are capable of creating something that works better for everyone. You can see it. You have a vision, one that nags at you. As a district leader, a school leader, or a member of a distributed leadership team, you feel in your bones the call for system shifts like the pull of waves in the ocean. However, let's be clear: the work you are doing in schools, the moral imperative of creating something that positively impacts all learners, is far more important and far more complex. The snorkeling anecdote illustrates that even small goals and small changes are difficult to make when we are committed to our routines. Changing how we educate our youth and educators is monumental, but there is a science behind it. We can take steps to realize our vision, but first, we must recognize the challenges we face and create a strategy for addressing those areas.

It may be helpful to recognize that two types of challenges require us to change: technical problems and adaptive challenges (Heifetz et al., 2009). Technical problems can be addressed through existing solutions and expert guidance. The barrier of identifying high-quality instructional materials is a technical problem that can be addressed by accessing research from organizations like EdReports and WhatWorks Clearinghouse and using curriculum alignment rubrics. These types of problems differ from adaptive challenges (e.g., learning how to get teachers to use instructional materials in ways that are inclusive, equitable, and promote deeper learning), which require leaders and stakeholders to collaboratively experiment with new procedures, norms, or beliefs to address problems of practice (Pak et al., 2020). A great example of an adaptive challenge as it relates to curriculum adoption was discussed by Pak and colleagues (2020) in the research paper "The Adaptive Challenges of Curriculum Implementation."

> It helps to adaptively uncover some of the root causes behind teachers' issues with these technical resources, as some of these root causes address teachers' mindsets about student ability and cultural interests (i.e., the adaptive challenge of speaking the unspeakable). . . .
>
> While there were teachers across all districts who appreciated the rigor of the provided curriculum for exposing them to the demands of the standards, there were also teachers who expressed that their students did not have the "prerequisite skills, prior knowledge, or background experience to keep up with the pacing" in the curricula (teacher interview, Orrington). Statements such as this reflect the fixed mindset that students' intelligence levels are static, rendering them unprepared to take on academic challenges (p. 8).

This example makes it clear that it would be much quicker to adopt a curriculum review rubric than to challenge ableist mindsets about student potential. The work of instructional leaders is to consistently work toward a shared vision while balancing and addressing our systems' technical and adaptive barriers (Table 1.1).

The book *UDL Playbook for School and District Leaders* (Novak and Woodlock, 2021) shares another example of how adaptive challenges will require much more than technical fixes and how it's the adaptive challenges that will require long-term commitment, passion, and patience.

> If you have a negative staff culture, you can't just pick up the phone and fix it. You can't read a blog online or show a video and solve it. There are no procedures addressing what to do when your staff feels hopeless, not listened to, and uninspired. Sure, you can host a morning coffee as a technical bandaid, but that won't solve your problem. Adaptive challenges will take every strength you have.

Table 1.1 Technical and adaptive challenges.

Technical Problem	Adaptive Challenge
It is easy to identify.	It is difficult to identify.
Most of the time has quick and easy solutions (tried and tested).	It requires changes in the way things are done (changes in approach to work).
It can be solved by expertise or authority generally.	People who are working from where the problem is generated need to solve it.
It requires small changes within organizational boundaries.	Requires changes in many places that may cross organizational boundaries.
People are receptive to technical solutions.	People resist acknowledging adaptive challenges.
Solutions can be implemented fast and by authority/experts.	Solutions emerge from experimentation and discovery, and take a long time to implement.

Source: Adapted from Heifetz et al. (2009).

Pause and Reflect

Brainstorm some of the challenges you are facing in your leadership practice as it relates to building a system that supports all learners. Are they technical problems or adaptive challenges?

Suppose you and your team have already completed an equity review or a district self-assessment. In that case, you may have begun to invest in necessary changes, but your district will not realize full implementation and complex change until all the systems are in place, and that work is not easy. We want you to feel confident in navigating the tides of systems change. We are here to charter this journey with you. When we finally build the multi-tiered system that our students, staff, families, and communities deserve, we can all celebrate with a snorkeling trip (bring your sunscreen and life preservers!).

The Need for Complex Change

The persistent achievement gap between privileged and nonprivileged populations has been referred to as the "most stubborn, perplexing issue confronting American schools today" (Evans, 2005, p. 582). Some researchers argue that the achievement and opportunity gaps are "an act of civil war" (Thirunarayanan, 2004, p. 479). We all know this needs to change. What is missing is concrete guidance on how to accomplish this.

Creating robust multi-tiered systems will require us to make significant changes to our systems and structures. Understanding change theory, therefore, is a helpful foundation for thinking about the work ahead. Understanding the bigger picture of how change occurs helps visualize the journey. In the following sections, we will unpack major change theories and make concrete connections to how these theories will impact your work in building comprehensive MTSS systems. Think of them as tools in your toolbox as you learn more about how to put theory into practice.

Unfreeze–Change–Refreeze Model

In 1947, Kurt Lewin theorized the unfreeze–change–refreeze model, which argued that for change to occur, practitioners have to reject and replace prior systems. "Prior systems" are the current beliefs, practices, and routines we must change. Turns out, this is much more difficult than one would think. The book *Unlearning: Changing Your Beliefs and Practices with UDL* (Posey and Novak, 2020) notes how difficult it is to unfreeze simple "facts" we think we understand. For example, it is a simple fact that when there is no light, there is no color.

When you look at an apple, it looks red because wavelengths of light are reflected from the apple onto the cone photoreceptors in your eyes. You perceive the redness because of the reflection of that light. Without light, there is no color. Literally, nothing is reflected onto the cones of your eyes, so there is nothing to perceive. No electrical signal goes to your brain.

Nothing is stimulated. However, regardless of these scientific facts, individuals who have been placed in a completely dark room, a room where absolutely no light can enter, still claim to see an apple as being red. They know that there is no light in the room and they have learned the science that explains how in an absence of light, there is no color. However, they still claim to see color. They use reasoning such as, "My eyes must not have adjusted to the dark yet so I could still see the redness," or "There must have been some light that somehow got into the room." They still see the apple as red even though it is impossible, simply because they believe the apple is red and beliefs and practices are hard to change. Too often in our systems, practices and procedures are followed because they were followed before. Consider the following responses:

- *That's how we have always done it.*
- *That's what the contract says.*
- *No one has ever questioned this before.*
- *Why are we suddenly changing everything?*

All of these responses come from individuals who are "frozen" in the current model. Sadly, the current model was not built for all students, and "freezing" there leads to the continuation of oppressive, inequitable, and exclusionary practices and systems.

Let's discuss a specific example. There are silos between general and special education in many schools and districts. Students who receive special education services are referred to as special education students, or more derogatory terms (e.g., sped) as opposed to recognizing that all students are general education students first, and serving students with disabilities is the responsibility of all teachers.

Many practitioners are "frozen" in thinking about special education as a location or a program instead of programming. Terms like "my kids," "your kids," and "those kids" are evidence of these silos. This mindset is so pervasive in the system that many educators do not challenge it. Simply, people are "frozen" in the belief that serving students with disabilities is the responsibility of the special education department. This needs to change. Shifting mindset is challenging and painful because it means acknowledging that current beliefs do not serve all learners.

Pause and Reflect

What are some places where your colleagues are "frozen?" Are there any places where you are "frozen" in your practices?

Change is possible, however, when we challenge mindsets and build systems that support collective teacher efficacy. What is problematic, however, is that when we can challenge and change mindsets, educators often "refreeze." This frequently occurs when educators acknowledge, "I used to think _____, but now I think _____." We need to take it a step further in our systems today and recognize, "In the future, I may think differently."

To build inclusive and equitable systems, we must be flexible enough to know that our work is ongoing and cyclical. For these reasons, we both strongly advocate that the "freeze" is unnecessary. We have to be open to change and ready to adapt when evidence suggests there is a better way to do things. We advocate for an unlearning process that supports a cycle of reflect-change-growth (see Figure 1.1).

Concerns-Based Adoption

To "unfreeze" mindsets that do not serve all learners, it is helpful to understand the concept of concerns-based adoption and how people experience change. Hall, Wallace, and Dossett (1973) proposed this model to outline the stages that people go through as they experience change and the corresponding questions that define each stage (see Table 1.2).

Pause and Reflect

As you reflect on the stages of the Concerns-Based Adoption Model, consider staff members who are in each stage. Where are you currently as it relates to creating an inclusive and equitable MTSS?

When a change in an organization is introduced, people learn about this change and naturally want to know more. Let's continue to explore the "frozen" mindset that students with disabilities are primarily the

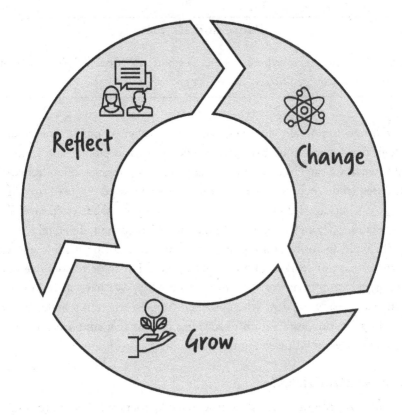

Figure 1.1   Reflect–change–growth cycle.

Table 1.2   Concerns-Based Adoption Model.

Stage	General Concern
Awareness	What is this change I've been hearing about?
Information	Tell me everything I need to know.
Personal	What does this mean for me?
Management	How will I manage all this?
Consequence	What will happen if I implement the change? What if I do not?
Collaboration	How can we help each other through this change?
Refocusing	How can we make this even better?

Source: Adapted from Hall and Loucks,1979.

responsibility of the special education department. As we build awareness of MTSS in our organizations, it must be clear that we need inclusive practices and placements. All students, including those with significant support needs, deserve equitable access to grade-level learning in general education classrooms with their peers.

A vision is necessary to build awareness, but it is not sufficient. All staff, including general and special educators, need a skill set that allows them to collaborate to meet the needs of all learners. All teachers need to build subject matter expertise, universally design instruction, incorporate best practices in social and emotional learning, design behavioral expectations that are culturally responsive, and design classrooms that are linguistically appropriate, culturally sustaining, and evidence-informed. In addition to these skills, special educators tailor specially designed instruction aligned to students' IEP goals. As we share information about MTSS, we have to be transparent about what it means to educators, their working relationships, and their job responsibilities.

As teachers learn more about the required changes, they ask, "How can I manage all this?" We must share how the system will support their collective efficacy at this stage. General and special educators need support to sustain healthy working relationships and co-teaching models. Without ongoing professional learning, instructional coaching, common planning, and strong systems for educator evaluation, educators will feel anxious, overwhelmed, and potentially ineffective. If we want to support the reflect-change-growth model, we need to provide high-quality professional learning experiences, high-quality instructional materials, and ongoing support.

As educators and former administrators, we both know that people aren't lining up begging for change. As we discussed with the unfreeze-change-refreeze model, change is painful. We have to incentivize change. Educators will ask, "Well, what happens if we do this?" We need to have an answer. For example, we can offer early adopters the opportunity to pilot new resources, opportunities to receive additional support in the form of a co-teaching partner or instructional coaching support, and/or the opportunity to become a part of a distributed leadership team, and so on. We need to help both general and special educators recognize that change is worthwhile; to do that, we must be strategic. If we just put up a banner that reads, "Everyone Change Now. It's the Right Thing to Do," we can expect some significant resistance.

At the consequence stage, it is also critical that we discuss what will happen if educators do not implement changes. This is not meant to be a time to dish out threats and punishments, but we need to create a robust accountability system to support the change. We need administrators to have radical candor and say, "Implementing inclusive practices and serving students with disabilities is not optional. If you struggle with this change, we will provide instructional coaching cycles, targeted feedback, and the necessary resources to increase your efficacy."

You may be reflecting on the Concerns-Based Adoption Model and thinking, "There is no way we can put all of this into place right away," which puts you in the Management Phase. Worry not! We will provide you with the necessary support and structure to move through this phase.

Implementation Science

Systems change requires us to address numerous elements. How do we create a strategic plan that addresses this? This is where the field of implementation science comes in. Implementation science is a term broadly used across several fields to describe how evidence-based programs are put into action to produce outcomes (Fixsen et al., 2005).

The Every Student Succeeds Act (ESSA, 2015) emphasizes the use of evidence-based activities, strategies, and interventions (collectively referred to as "interventions"). The term *evidence-based* means an intervention that demonstrates a statistically significant effect on improving student outcomes or other relevant outcomes. Unless otherwise specified, *evidence-based* means meets any of the four evidence levels described next. The criteria for identifying "evidence-based" interventions based on each of ESSA's four levels are as follows:

- Strong evidence from at least one well-designed and well-implemented experimental study
- Moderate evidence from at least one well-designed and well-implemented quasi-experimental study
- Promising evidence from at least one well-designed and well-implemented correlational study with statistical controls for selection bias
- Demonstrating a rationale based on high-quality research findings or positive evaluation that such activity, strategy, or intervention is

likely to improve student outcomes or other relevant outcomes; and includes ongoing efforts to examine the effects of such activity, strategy, or intervention

The National Implementation Research Network (NIRN) conducted a meta-analysis of more than 800 articles related to implementation practices to devise a model of implementation science, which can be simplified in the equation: effective interventions × effective implementation = improved outcomes (Fixsen et al., 2013). Ensuring that effective interventions are evidence-based is necessary for improved outcomes, but not sufficient. As the equation suggests, we need effective implementation as well.

As consultants, we have worked with countless districts that want to change and know what effective interventions to put in place, but they struggle with creating a strategy for effective implementation. Implementation science builds on the Concerns-Based Adoption Model by identifying specific elements, or drivers, necessary to build a multi-tiered system that is flexible enough to provide all learners with what they need when they need it. There are three systems drivers, which include numerous elements that drive systems change:

- *Leadership drivers* focus on providing the right leadership strategies for different leadership challenges. A successful MTSS system requires leaders who are committed to creating inclusive environments where all students can be successful academically, behaviorally, socially, and emotionally. Important leadership considerations include scheduling, resource allocation, creating an inclusive culture and climate, and engaging all stakeholders in the work. Leadership drivers address the development of a vision, strategic planning, family and community engagement, staffing, and resource allocation. Implementation requires leaders who address the adaptive issues (such as identifying barriers and removing them and consensus building) paired with technical support (such as finding time and resources).
- *Competency drivers* are elements that help educators build the skill set necessary to support all learners. Competency drivers revolve around building educator capacity to affect positive student outcomes through thoughtful staffing models, offering high-quality

professional development models, research-based coaching strategies, aligned educator evaluation models, and the development of fidelity assessments and feedback loops to monitor progress. When competency drivers are in place, educators feel prepared to design and deliver equitable and inclusive instruction academically, behaviorally, socially, emotionally, culturally, and linguistically. Teachers who receive substantial professional development—an average of 49 hours a year—can boost their students' achievement by about 21 percentile points (Yoon et al., 2007). It should be noted that the quality of PD and its focus have more impact than the hours or "dosage" (Kraft, Blazar, and Hogan, 2018). Additionally, recent research notes that the ongoing training must be collaborative, extended over a prolonged period, and supplemented with instructional coaching (Smith and Robinson, 2020).

- *Implementation drivers* help systems create and sustain environments for effective educational services. These include safe schools, high-quality instructional materials, a system that supports data-based decision-making, schedules that provide adequate time for common planning and student services, and creating a robust assessment framework that aligns with the overall tiered system of support.

We have used these drivers for years, forming the basis of many of our materials and resources. In this book, we layer these drivers into a framework that is more overtly equity-focused and rooted in deeper learning. Figure 1.2 provides an image of this updated framework (Massachusetts Department of Elementary and Secondary Education, Commonwealth Consulting, and Novak Educational Consulting, 2022). To learn more about this work, created in collaboration with the Massachusetts Department of Elementary and Secondary Education, a Coherence Guidebook and companion self-assessment are publicly available on the department's website at www.doe.mass.edu/csdp/guidebook (Massachusetts Department of Elementary and Secondary Education, 2023a).

In this deeper learning model for MTSS, all drivers are present, but we have reorganized them into more student-centered categories. In this framework, we look at the instructional design that students experience as well as their sense of belonging and agency. We are also more keenly aware of the need to integrate equitable practices into our systems design. Table 1.3 includes a crosswalk between the implementation of science-based drivers and deeper learning systems components. The crosswalk

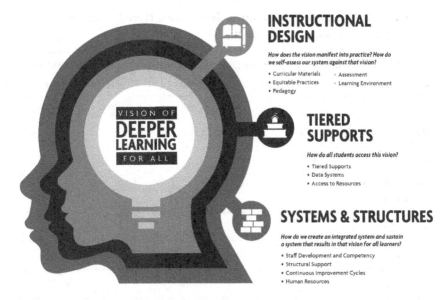

Figure 1.2   Deeper learning model for MTSS.

includes all implementation drivers as well as additional elements to create a more robust and student-centered approach.

Changing our systems is a multiyear process. Fixsen and colleagues (2005) argue that the changes take at least four years, which is why it is so critical to have a strategic action plan that supports us as we work toward a vision of inclusive and equitable MTSS. Building a system with the necessary drivers happens in stages, with districts moving from an exploration phase to installation, initial implementation, and finally full implementation (see Figure 1.3).

Exploration. The goal of the exploration stage is to identify the need for change, learn about possible innovations that may drive change, develop a team to support the work as it progresses through the stages, and assess and create readiness for change.

Installation. Once the team decides to move forward, the installation phase secures the support necessary to put innovative approaches into practice (i.e., pilot sites), develops feedback loops to streamline communication and measure effectiveness, and creates an action plan for initial implementation.

Initial implementation. In this stage, teams gather data using feedback loops to measure the impact of implementation and develop improvement strategies based on the data. Implementation supports are refined based on evidence to ensure maximum impact.

Table 1.3 Implementation science and tiered framework of deeper learning crosswalk.

Equitable MTSS Practices	Leadership Driver	Competency Driver	Implementation Driver
Vision			
Instructional Vision			
Instructional Design			
Curriculum Materials			X
Equitable Practices			
Pedagogy		X	
Assessment		X	X
Learning Environment			
Tiered Systems			
Tiered Supports			X
Data-Driven			X
Access to Resources	X		
Systems and Structures			
Staff Development and Competency		X	
Structural Systems	X		
Continuous Improvement Cycles	X		
Human Resources		X	

Full implementation. In this stage, the implementation of innovations and solutions has scaled throughout the organization. Because of its documented impact on student outcomes, drivers are well-integrated and routinely and effectively supported by ongoing professional learning, resources, and administrative support.

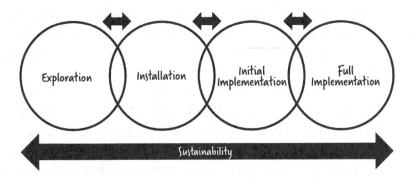

Figure 1.3   Phases of implementation science.

Pause and Reflect

What is your current stage in your MTSS change process?

Improvement Science

As we build more inclusive and equitable systems through implementation science, we want to ensure that the drivers we put in place positively impact our work and move us closer to our vision of meeting the needs of all learners. First, let's unpack the core components of systems improvement. There are six core principles of improvement outlined in *Learning to Improve: How America's Schools Can Get Better at Getting Better* (Bryk, Gomez, Grunow, and LeMahieu, 2015; Carnegie Foundation for the Advancement of Teaching, 2019) and summarized here:

- Make the work problem-specific and user-centered. Districts and schools need to articulate the problems they are trying to solve (e.g., achievement gaps, disproportionality) by using data as well as a comprehensive self-assessment process so it's clear how an action plan will address areas of need.
- Variation in performance is the core problem to address. Each district and school works well for some students, but our current systems do not increase the outcomes of all learners. As a result, an MTSS implevmentation team must build a clear understanding of how the variation in performance can be addressed through thoughtful

improvement planning. It is critical to remember that no single intervention or program will work for all learners. The implementation
team must use data to determine what will work for specific students
under a set of conditions.

- See the system that produces the current outcomes. It is hard to
  improve what you do not fully understand, so an understanding of
  root causes is critical when improvement planning. Understanding
  root causes allows a district or school to create a theory of action, or
  a hypothesis of how specific action steps will address problem areas.

- We cannot improve at scale what we cannot measure. Improving the
  outcomes of students requires a robust system of data that is consistently reviewed throughout the improvement process.

- Anchor practice improvement in disciplined inquiry. Implementation teams need to meet frequently to reflect on data "to learn
  fast, fail fast, and improve quickly" (Carnegie Foundation for the
  Advancement of Teaching, 2019). Having time scheduled to review
  data and refine improvement efforts is critical to increase the outcomes of all learners.

- Accelerate improvements through networked communities. District
  and school administrators must "embrace the wisdom of crowds"
  (Carnegie Foundation for the Advancement of Teaching, 2019).
  When implementation teams include multiple stakeholders and are
  committed to distributed leadership and elevating and celebrating
  the voices of all members, improvement is possible.

Keep these principles of improvement in mind as you learn more about
improvement science. Meeting the needs of all learners will not happen
overnight but when a committed team is committed to the process of
improvement, we can create a system where all students have equal opportunities to succeed.

Pause and Reflect

Reflect on the six core components of improvement and determine your
organization's alignment with the core principles. Note any areas of strength
as well as areas that will be important to address during the strategic planning process. In short, how will you improve your improvement process?

Improvement science is helpful as we navigate this journey. Improvement science is a methodology that focuses on adopting an evidence-based approach that aims to improve practice using cycles of inquiry. A publication from the National Implementation Research Network notes the relationship between implementation science and improvement science (McColskey-Leary and Garman-McClaine, 2021, p. 2).

> Implementation science and improvement science have both been leveraged to increase students' academic, behavioral, and social emotional outcomes. Implementation science emphasizes integrating implementation supports (e.g., training, coaching, teams, leadership) to move evidence-based practices into routine use. Furthermore, implementation science often starts with exploration activities, including identifying the need for a new practice or structures to support existing programs and creating readiness and buy-in. On the other hand, improvement science typically begins with a specific problem of practice that requires addressing. Improvement science—a methodology that focuses on improving practice—efforts are undertaken by a data-driven approach that aims to improve general practice, using cycles of inquiry systematically (e.g., plan-do-study-act [PDSA] cycles). . . .
>
> Both sciences (a) rely heavily on data to assess their respective outcomes of interest, (b) focus on improving systems, (c) simultaneously address policy and practice, (d) use improvement cycles, and (e) attend to practitioner-level needs. Differences between improvement science and implementation science, however, should be highlighted. Primarily, improvement science is problem-specific and user-focused, while implementation science is context and practice concentrated. Both sciences focus on enhancing the use (adoption, implementation, and sustainment) of effective practices or programs to improve outcomes for students.

The Institute of Educational Sciences, a project of the US Department of Education (2017), notes, "Improvement science is a problem-solving approach centered on continuous inquiry and learning. Change ideas are tested in rapid cycles, resulting in efficient and useful feedback to inform system improvements." This comes full circle with our proposed model of reflect-change-growth. As leaders, we need to create rapid feedback loops to ensure that as we work toward our strategic vision, we get positive returns on our investments. We need to know what works quickly, so we can continue it while also recognizing what doesn't work yet, so we can make necessary changes.

Improvement science helps districts understand how to focus on specific problems, introduce small measurable changes, measure the impact of these changes, and determine whether and when these changes create true improvements that should be spread more widely across the system. Improvement science is often defined by these six tasks (Aguilar, Nayfack, and Bush-Mecenas, 2017):

- Identify specific problems
- Focus on key participants
- Attend to variation in performance (what works, for whom, under what set of conditions)
- Reflect upon the existing system that is designed to produce current outcomes (systems thinking)
- Measure processes and outcomes to assess the efficacy of strategies
- Utilize rapid Plan-Do-Study-Act (PDSA) cycles to promote quick improvement

The PDSA cycle is a four-step process that is useful in guiding continuous improvement to test an evidence-based practice in your setting. During the planning stage, teams reflect on the problem of practice and evidence-based solutions and create a theory of action. A theory of action provides a logical, organized set of ideas to guide the intended work of the educational system to achieve the desired results. Theories of action are commonly described using a series of "if. . .then" statements. For example, "If we [implement this framework], then [this will be the change in practice], so [these are the outcomes we anticipate]."

The Rhode Island Department of Education (n.d.) uses the template to share an exemplar of the theory of action: *If* we implement strategies to improve the culture and climate of our school, including restorative justice practices, *then* teachers and administrators will enhance their relationships with students and use more effective conflict resolution techniques, *so* students will feel more positively about their school experience and spend more time engaged in instruction.

Pause and Reflect

Use the template to create a theory of action about MTSS in your school or district: If we build a comprehensive MTSS then [this will be the change in practice], so [these are the outcomes we anticipate].

The next step in PSDA is "do," which requires teams to implement an action plan aligned to the theory of action and begin to collect data. Using the sample theory of action shown earlier, teams would determine how to measure student perception about their school experience (e.g., student surveys) and time spent engaged in instruction so the measures can be used to determine impact. During the study step, participants examine data and reflect on the effectiveness of the intervention. During this step, the Improvement Team compares the data with the predictions or hypotheses put forward in the theory of action to see whether there are signs of progress toward the aim or if the team needs to revise the plan accordingly.

The last step of the PSDA process is to act. This step integrates learning generated throughout the process, which can be used to adjust strategies or make changes to the plan. Often, multiple PDSA cycles are necessary to determine whether a change in practice results in intended outcomes.

Improvement science requires us to be vigilant and create PDSA cycles where we continually self-assess, explore outcomes using multiple means, and report those outcomes in collaborative, transparent, and culturally and linguistically appropriate ways. In short, we can't get "frozen" in our action plan if we aren't making the desired impact on the students we serve.

Summary

The chapter discussed numerous change models, and all of these will help to build an equitable MTSS that serves all learners. We need to ensure students and educators get the support they need academically, behaviorally, socially, and emotionally to succeed. MTSS requires complex organizational change, the development of implementation supports or drivers (i.e., implementation science), and a systems-wide data-driven approach with feedback loops (i.e., improvement science) within a framework of deeper learning. This book intends to take you on a journey to do just that.

Reflection Questions

1. We discussed the unfreeze-change-refreeze model. Reflect on your current system and identify mindsets, skill sets, and/or practices where colleagues are "frozen." How have you addressed these "frozen" elements in your practice?

2. The Concerns-Based Adoption Model requires us to support educators as they ask, "What happens if we do this?" and "What happens if we do not?" Take time and prepare your answers to those questions as it relates to equitable MTSS.

3. What is the value of shifting MTSS into a model that centers on the student experience and equity?

4. In implementation science, the first stage is Exploration, where stakeholders identify the need for change. Take a moment and consider what you believe needs to change in your system to meet the needs of all learners.

5. Improvement science requires that we respond to multiple data forms. In your own practice, what data do you examine and triangulate consistently to determine the effectiveness of current practices?

2 | Understanding MTSS

In this chapter, we define MTSS and discuss how critical it is to ensure that all learners have access to Tier 1 instruction that challenges them, supports them, and affirms their identity while ensuring supplemental supports are also available when students need them. We also discuss the components, or ingredients, of a comprehensive MTSS system that can create the conditions necessary for inclusive, equitable, and deeper learning for all students.

Baking, Not Caking

MTSS is a noun, not a verb. We can't even count how many times we have said that in the last year, often in response to "We are already doing MTSS." But MTSS is not something to do; rather, it is a system you build to ensure that all learners have equitable access to Tier 1 instruction that meets their needs while also getting additional support when necessary. Thinking about MTSS in this way is a significant shift for many educators.

Let's share an analogy. Neither of us is a particularly talented baker, but we can certainly follow a recipe. If you gave us a recipe to make a layered carrot cake with cream cheese frosting, we could definitely present you with a finished product, although it might be more reminiscent of the cooking show *Nailed It*, where home bakers with a terrible track record try to re-create edible masterpieces. The results are hilarious.

In this scenario, we would be baking a cake but not "caking." The same is true with MTSS. We do not "do" it, but rather, we look to build it by ensuring we have the necessary ingredients, or drivers, as well as the strategies to put those ingredients into place. This recipe, or blueprint, can guide us in building a multi-tiered system. And yes, as you build it, you may experience some *Nailed It* fails, but by creating feedback loops and aligning your work to improvement science, you will be able to course-correct quickly and efficiently.

Defining MTSS

MTSS is a system designed to meet the needs of all students by ensuring that schools optimize data-driven decision-making, progress monitoring, and evidence-based supports and strategies with increasing intensity to sustain student growth academically, behaviorally, and social emotionally. MTSS is recommended in the Every Student Succeeds Act (ESSA) as a "comprehensive continuum of evidence-based, systemic practices to support a rapid response to students' needs, with regular observation to facilitate data-based instructional decision making."

At its heart, according to the Council of Great City Schools (2012), MTSS is a self-repeating, self-correcting, ongoing methodology for effective decision-making at all levels of the system and across all three tiers. We need MTSS in our schools so that we can minimize or eliminate barriers and improve student outcomes by designing equitable, tiered, universally designed systems of support that address needs in ways that are culturally sustaining. It is a system for educating all of our students and educating each of them completely as a "whole" person. To realize this success, multi-tiered systems must be supported by drivers to ensure that all district resources are focused on supporting our students, who can and will learn and succeed with our support. Harlacher et al. (2014) described six key tenets of the MTSS framework:

- All students are capable of grade-level learning with adequate support.
- MTSS is rooted in proactivity and prevention.
- The system utilizes evidence-based practices.

- Decisions and procedures are driven by school and student data.
- The degree of support given to each student is based on their needs.
- Implementation occurs schoolwide and requires stakeholder collaboration.

Given the importance of evidence-based practices and data culture in MTSS, it may be valuable to pause to reflect on your district's current focus on evidence-based practice. We offered the following prompts in our book *Universally Designed Leadership* (Novak and Rodriguez, 2016, p. 21). It may be valuable to share these questions with your team as you build MTSS:

- What are your current feelings about how this district uses data to impact instruction? Please be candid in your response.
- What specific steps would we need to take to make data conversations more meaningful in your school or department?
- What barriers do we face if we want all stakeholders to have important conversations about data and how that data impacts instruction?
- Please describe the culture of your school or department. What would need to change in your culture in order for all parties to embrace evidence-based decision-making?
- What ongoing professional development would we need to support a culture of evidence-based decision-making in our district?
- What would all leaders need to understand in order to support evidence-based decision-making in our district?

In our own work as district leaders, these questions yielded valuable evidence about our district's data culture, which helped us better understand MTSS. Research suggests the result of full MTSS implementation when districts are committed to evidence-based practices and a culture of data is that every student engages in the general education curriculum with a flexible master schedule, flexible staffing, and three tiers of intensity of instruction directed to academics, behavior, and social emotional learning and significantly greater percentages of students achieve at grade level (Choi, McCart, and Sailor, 2020; Council of Great City Schools, 2012. MTSS is not just about tiered interventions but how all the school or district systems fit together to ensure a high-quality education for all students. That said, students have access to a continuum of tiered supports based on needs.

Baking a cake is also a helpful analogy when thinking about MTSS because of its multiple tiers or continuum of tiered supports. What makes a layered cake so darn impressive is how the layers build on each other. When you have three sponge cakes cooling in round pans on the stovetop, they are simply three different cakes. Building them on top of each other makes the real showstopper; the same is true in our schools and districts.

Multi-tiered support systems are intended to meet the needs of all learners, including students with disabilities and those who need additional challenges. All students should receive Tier 1 support. Tier 2 and Tier 3 supports are not intended to replace Tier 1 supports. At different points in their educational journey, any one student may need the support in Tiers 2 and 3 and should have equitable access to these. For example, if a student needs a service and they do not "qualify" due to predetermined constructs, we must examine whether our structures are effectively designed to foster student success. If students cannot access the support they need, as soon as they need it, and instead have to fail to make progress before getting additional assistance, our system has not produced its intended results.

Pause and Reflect

In your school or district, can all students get the supports they need academically, behaviorally, socially, and emotionally as soon as they need them? Do they receive these supports in addition to Tier 1 instruction or are they pulled out from that instruction to receive support?

Before diving into additional tiers, let's unpack a case study of what inclusive Tier 1 looks like in practice. In the MTSS Blueprint we created in partnership with the Massachusetts Department of Elementary and Secondary Education, we shared a "Case in Point" to describe how Tier 1 can be designed to better meet the needs of all learners (Massachusetts Department of Education, Novak Educational Consulting, Commonwealth Consulting Agency, 2019).

In many classrooms, teachers design a "one-size-fits-all" academic curriculum for learners. For example, when designing instruction, many teachers expect students to read printed text like novels, primary source documents, and/or textbooks to learn content and then answer questions about the content using textual evidence in predictable formats, like the five-paragraph essay. Printed materials result in barriers for some students, who may not be able to access the text because they cannot decode at that level, have visual impairments, or are English learners. In a universally designed high school classroom, students may have options about which texts to read, or they may be encouraged to choose a novel based on interest, that is relevant, authentic, and meaningful as they work to meet the standard. If reading the same text, students may have the option to read the hard copy or access the text online, where they can customize the display of information, listen to the text, or use translation tools. When eliciting students' understanding of the text, teachers may ask questions at different depths of knowledge and encourage students to answer in writing or through a short presentation, in an infographic, or through video or audio mediums. As they are working, students may have access to multiple materials such as exemplars, sentence stems, graphic organizers, highlighters, peer-editing, and writing conferences with the teacher. When students have options and choices to access texts and express what they have learned in more flexible ways, they can be educated together in an inclusive classroom, regardless of variability.

When Tier 1 is designed with inclusive and equitable practices, all students can access instruction in Tier 1 classrooms. Student assessments such as universal screeners, statewide assessments, curriculum-based assessments, and diagnostic assessments can be jointly analyzed to help provide information that schools can use to determine the level of support a student needs, whether that is Tier 1 only, or additional supports from Tier 2 or 3.

Tier 2 provides more intensive, targeted, and supplemental support to students. We cannot overstate how important it is that this support occurs in addition to Tier 1. We repeatedly say, "Supplement, not supplant" when working with educators. In 2020, the National Center on Educational Outcomes (NCEO) and the TIES Center jointly published a report, "MTSS for All: Including Students with the Most Significant Cognitive Disabilities" (Thurlow et al., 2020). The report notes (p. 1):

[MTSS] is a framework for organizing and providing a tiered instructional continuum to support learning for all students. MTSS has the potential to meet the academic and behavioral needs of all students. Unfortunately, students with the most significant cognitive disabilities often are not included in this framework even though they should be. When a group of students with disabilities is not included in an MTSS framework, the foundational concept of all students being general education students first, with special education services supplementary, is eroded.

Tier 2 interventions are generally done in small groups and include additional opportunities to practice the skills necessary for core instruction or strategies for enrichment. Tier 2 services are defined by student needs drawn from data collection. We generally like to split Tier 2 into Tier 2A and Tier 2B.

Tier 2A is often an intervention offered in the classroom by the teacher using the intervention materials built into the core curriculum. This intervention time is in addition to core instructional time. This may occur during an intervention block or a "What I Need" (WIN) block outside core instruction. For example, in the WIN block, a teacher may work with a small group of students to provide access to grade-level text using the intervention sections or to focus on standards-based skill acceleration activities.

Tier 2B interventions are also targeted but less at the curriculum level and more at the individual skill level. They may also occur during an intervention, flex, or What I Need (WIN) block. An interventionist or specialist often provides these interventions. The supports and services provided in Tier 2B use an evidence-based intervention program where the length, duration, and staffing ratio are programmatically defined.

Pause and Reflect

Does your school or district distinguish between Tier 2A and 2B? What may be the impact of supporting colleagues to differentiate between the two?

Tier 3 provides more intensive support. These are often explicit, focused, evidence-based interventions that occur individually or in very small groups that are often specially designed. Tier 3 is not synonymous with special education. For example, students with disabilities should not be excluded from Tier 1 and 2 services; likewise, students without disabilities should not be excluded from Tier 3 services. At different points in their educational journey, any one student may need the support in Tiers 2 and 3 and should have equitable access to these. We must be conscientious about not labeling or siloing students according to their needs. Similarly, tiers are not placements or designations that follow students throughout their academic careers.

For example, a student may receive Tier 1 support in a classroom, Tier 2 reading support during an intervention block, and Tier 3 counseling services for social emotional support regardless of whether the student has an IEP, a 504, or a behavior plan. A student who receives these supports is not a "Tier 2" or a "Tier 3" student but has access to reading support in Tier 2 and social emotional support in Tier 3, which mitigates barriers that may prevent the student from accessing support in Tier 1.

MTSS is much more than its tiered supports, so it is important to differentiate between MTSS and RTI. Response to Intervention (RTI) was added to the Individuals with Disabilities Education Act in 2004 as an alternative evaluation procedure. The goal of RTI was to provide screening for all students, deliver academic interventions, monitor student progress, and use the student responses to those interventions as a basis for determining special education eligibility (Turse and Albrecht, 2015).

ESSA distinctly references multi-tiered support systems, but there is no reference to Response to Intervention (RTI); they are two distinct tiered approaches. While RTI focuses on direct services, supports, and interventions for at-risk students, MTSS is a systematic approach that addresses conditions for creating successful and sustainable system change while supporting students and staff. Whereas RTI systems were built on a foundation of data-based decision-making, multi-tiered systems enhance the one-dimensional triangle by incorporating six foundational components: problem-solving, data-driven decision-making, instructional strategies, classroom management, curriculum design, and professional development (Dulaney, Hallam, and Wall, 2013). Rather than a reactive model responding to student achievement declines as a rationale for resources and services, MTSS puts the onus on the system, not the student, and is proactive in getting all students what they need.

The California Department of Education (2021) highlights the differences between the two frameworks. They argue that MTSS has a broader scope than an RTI because MTSS also includes:

- Focusing on aligning the entire system of initiatives, supports, and resources
- Promoting district participation in identifying and supporting systems for alignment of resources, as well as site and grade level
- Systematically addressing support for all students, including gifted and high achievers
- Enabling a paradigm shift for providing support and setting higher expectations for all students through intentional design and redesign of integrated services and supports, rather than a selection of a few components of RTI and intensive interventions
- Endorsing Universal Design for Learning instructional strategies so all students have opportunities for learning through differentiated content, processes, and product
- Integrating instructional and intervention support so that systemic changes are sustainable and based on CCSS-aligned classroom instruction
- Challenging all school staff to change the way in which they have traditionally worked across all school settings

---

Pause and Reflect

In your school or district, is there a clear understanding of the differences between MTSS and RTI? If not, how can you begin to support educators and other stakeholders to recognize the differences?

Given the scope of the work, building an equitable MTSS requires multiple ingredients. As you reflect on the following ingredients, consider which are in place in your system already and which are not present yet. Later in the book, we will guide you through an MTSS self-assessment process. This exercise is simply an opportunity to build a shared understanding of all the components of MTSS. In addition to having a clear vision for

MTSS, we categorized the MTSS ingredients into three drivers: instructional design, tiered systems, and systems and structures.

Vision

The instructional vision is the guiding light for all the work to follow. It is the beacon of what we want to occur in all educational settings all of the time. It is a collective definition of strong and effective instructional practice. One of the most important responsibilities of any leader is establishing a vision and inviting others to share in its development. This is critical because, "If you do not have a common, agreed-on destination, then everyone is left to his or her own devices to imagine one—a scenario that results in unharnessed and unfocused efforts, with everyone believing that what he or she is doing is right. A common understanding of the destination allows all stakeholders to align their improvement efforts" (Gabriel and Farmer, 2009). Elements of vision in an MTSS model include a shared vision grounded in equity and the student experience.

Instructional Design

Instructional design is the heartbeat of our classrooms. In this component, we are utilizing high-quality instructional materials, engaging in equitable practices to support all learners, using effective pedagogical practices, ensuring that assessment information drives our work, and designing a learning environment that meets the needs of all learners. Table 2.1 identifies the subcategories of the instructional design component. We will explore these subcategories later in the text.

Tiered Systems

Tiered systems are designed to make sure that all students can access robust instructional design in all three domains as well as additional support when they need it. The three domains are defined here:

- **Academic domain:** The design of academic instruction should allow all students to have equitable access to grade-level standards in learning experiences that are engaging and personalized to their needs. Academic instruction in an MTSS system integrates evidence-based practices in all content areas so students can make

Table 2.1   Elements of instructional design in an MTSS model.

Curricular Materials	Equitable Practices	Pedagogy	Assessment	Learning Environment
• High-quality instructional materials • Coherence • Vision alignment	• Equitable access • Multilingual learner support • Students with disabilities/504 support	• Evidence-based instructional practice • Effective implementation • High expectations	• Data-informed practice • Data-informed decision-making • Engagement	• Safety • Belonging • Feedback

effective progress. Engaging all students in academic work is critical to implementing the state curriculum frameworks. Students must be actively involved in academic learning using evidence-based curriculum and pedagogical strategies. All students need time to engage in rigorous academic work, because this access is a primary predictor of student achievement.

■ **Behavioral domain:** Tiered behavioral systems use primary, secondary, and tertiary levels of support to provide an instructive approach to behavior, as opposed to more reactive models. Because it is systematic and comprehensive, tiered behavioral systems offer schools a structured approach to identify students who may be at risk, and provide increasingly intensive support for those who need it.

■ **Social-emotional domain:** Social emotional learning is built around social and emotional competencies: self-awareness, self-management, responsible decision-making, relationship skills, and social awareness. When schools and districts focus on supporting each student's social and emotional development, they provide options for students to self-regulate and access rigorous and engaging curriculum and instruction.

Pause and Reflect

As you consider the practices in your school or district, are academic, behavioral, and social and emotional needs equally important? If so, how do you know? If not, what adaptive changes may be necessary to ensure that all stakeholders are focused on the whole child and student experience in school?

In the components of tiered systems, we focus on tiered support across all three tiers and across all three domains, building robust data systems that drive support provided to students and access to resources such as staffing or scheduling to meet the needs of all learners. Table 2.2 summarizes the elements within the three main components of tiered systems.

Systems and Structures

The only way for all students to access robust instructional design and tiered support is to design systems and structures that make this happen. Districts must recognize the systemic barriers that prevent all students from accessing first, best instruction as well as additional support while also focusing on systems drivers such as staff competency, data culture, feedback loops, and human resources. Table 2.3 includes elements that support systems and structures.

Table 2.2   Elements of tiered systems in an equitable MTSS model.

Tiered Support	Data-Driven	Access to Resources
• Domains (Academic, Behavioral, Social Emotional)	• Data Systems	• Programmatic Reviews/Audits
• Tiered Interventions	• Assessment Plans	• Tiered Staffing
• Multilingual Support	• Data-Driven Culture	• Tiered Scheduling
• Support for Students with Disabilities	• Student Need Focus	• Community Partnerships
• Family/Caregiver Engagement		• Technology

Table 2.3 Elements of systems and structures in an equitable MTSS model.

Staff Development and Competency	Data-Driven	Continuous Improvement Cycles	Human Resources
• Professional learning plan • High-quality professional learning • Collaborative planning • Observation and feedback • Evaluation	• Vision alignment • Fiscal support • Structural review • Technology	• Leadership commitment • Continuous improvement • Representation from all stakeholders • Equity focused • Multiyear planning • Midcourse corrections and continuous improvement	• Distributive leadership • Hiring • Retention

As you have learned, numerous components need to be addressed to create an inclusive and equitable MTSS that supports all students. Although it seems like there are a lot of components, know that they are interconnected and that MTSS brings all evidence-based work together.

One analogy that may be helpful in thinking about the interconnectedness of the components is the game of basketball. During MTSS training, we sometimes show a highlight reel of Larry Bird, a player for the Boston Celtics (forgive us—we are Boston girls!). When he was in his prime, he was one of the greatest basketball players in the world. He was incredibly versatile, a fierce competitor, and a smart player. We ask participants to get in groups and watch the highlight reel together, noting all the different components of his game. Teams collaborate and often come up with a list that includes shooting, dunking, rebounding, passing, play calling, stealing, dribbling with both hands, his ability to jump high, his speed, and his knowledge of players on the court. Former players and coaches have much longer lists, but you get the picture. Once the lists are complete, it looks like a lot of different skills. At this point, we ask, "This is still basketball, right?" Participants laugh, but they begin to understand where we are going with this analogy. Larry Bird needed all of those skills to be a competitive basketball player. Even though a coach may choose to focus on a single skill or strategy in practice, it doesn't mean that the others aren't important. Based on game performance, the coach prioritizes training. The same is true in our districts.

If we are going to create an inclusive and equitable MTSS, we have to address a lot of components. In a particular improvement cycle, we may prioritize one component, but it is always important to remember how they connect and how a focus on one does not mean that another is not important. In the sport of MTSS, we need lots of drivers to best meet the needs of the learners we serve.

In the fall of 2018, we worked with a district in western Massachusetts. As we supported them in their MTSS journey, they recognized all the components they needed to address. The district team took stock of their district improvement efforts and recognized that if they were going to meet their long-term goals of dramatically increasing grade-level proficiency in reading and math and addressing each student's academic, social emotional, and behavioral needs through universal core instruction, they needed a unifying framework to guide their work. The district's receiver/superintendent wanted to take an MTSS approach, but it was important to ensure that MTSS was the unifying framework that brought all of their improvement efforts together. MTSS allowed the district leadership to have a common vision and understanding of how to prioritize work and mobilize departments to collaborate.

The district has been using the MTSS framework to make informed, collaborative decisions and set priorities and strategies. Just like the Celtics, the coaches and trainers need to prioritize skills and create a game plan, but it always comes back to being better at the game of basketball. Although the work is still in progress, this district is taking a deliberate and coordinated approach to MTSS implementation and applying their learning along the way. We hope to support you in doing the same.

Summary

In this chapter, we unpacked how MTSS is a system designed to meet the needs of all students by ensuring that districts optimize data-driven decision-making, progress monitoring, and evidence-based supports and strategies with increasing intensity to sustain student growth academically, behaviorally, socially, and emotionally. To build an inclusive and equitable MTSS, systems need numerous ingredients, or drivers, to ensure that no barriers exist to prevent all students from reaching their full potential. Later chapters will unpack each of the ingredients so you can better understand the strengths of your district or school as well as areas of need. This will drive an improvement process that creates equitable outcomes for all learners.

Reflection Questions

1. How did the discussion of MTSS in this chapter relate to your current understanding of MTSS in your school or district?
2. Does your school or district embrace "Supplement, not supplant," or are students pulled from Tier 1 instruction to get additional support? What barriers prevent students from receiving Tier 1 instruction with their peers if this is the case?
3. How is MTSS different from RTI? Why is it important to support educators in understanding similarities and differences?
4. How did the basketball analogy help you to see UDL as a unifying framework that brings all your improvement efforts together?

3 | The Power of Inclusive Practices

In this chapter, we focus on creating inclusive and equitable Tier 1 learning environments for all students by focusing on inclusive practice, Universal Design for Learning (UDL), differentiated instruction, and deeper learning. One of our favorite sayings is "You can't intervention your way out of weak Tier 1." Throughout this chapter, we discuss the components of an evidence-based Tier 1 classroom that supports multiple tasks and formats while diverse students work toward grade-level standards by engaging in authentic tasks.

The Power of Carrot Cake (Katie)

I love carrot cake. Ever since I was little, I have requested it on my birthday. To me, carrot cake is best when it's a whole meal. Think carrots, pineapple, walnuts, and cream cheese. When it's done right, it weighs a ton! When I'm introducing myself, I do not often lead with my love of carrot cake, but in a presentation last year, I did.

I kicked off a session on MTSS with an optimistic opener, inspired by CASEL's (2019) "3 Signature Practices Playbook." The playbook offers "practical ways to introduce and broaden the use of SEL practices in classrooms, schools, and workplaces." I used the Mix and Mingle activity, which builds community by encouraging participants to interact with each other, and sets the expectation that everyone's thinking and voice are valued. Below are the steps if you want to replicate the activity, and then I promise I'll get back to the carrot cake.

Since I was introducing MTSS using the baking analogy, I used the Mix and Mingle optimistic opening activity with this prompt: "What is your favorite dessert or treat that reminds you of your come-from place?" The use of "come-from place" is intentional not to exclude anyone who wasn't raised in what they would consider a home. On my card, I wrote "carrot cake." As a part of the mingle, I chatted with a superintendent in

---

Mix and Mingle Welcoming Activity (CASEL, 2019, p. 16)

On a card or half-sheet of paper, ask participants to write down a response to a prompt you give related to the topic at hand. (Begin with a low-vulnerability prompt, such as "What did you do for fun yesterday?" or "What have you read or watched recently that you enjoyed?" or something connected to upcoming work like "What's one thing you already know about [insert your content]?")

1. When you announce, "Mix and mingle!" and turn on music, participants move around.
2. When the music stops, participants find a partner near them. Help with pairing if needed.
3. Partners share their responses, listen actively to each other, and ask follow-up questions.
4. Start the music again and repeat the sequence with another partner or two, as your time permits.

   Debrief by asking one or more of these questions:

- What were some of the things you appreciate about doing this activity?
- What was challenging about it?
- What SEL skills did you use?

a district in Vermont and shared details about my mother-in-law's famous recipe. When the timer was up, the session continued. A year later, that same superintendent invited me to his district to work with his amazing leadership team to support them in their MTSS needs assessment process. I was happy to be included in the meeting. When I arrived, however, he shared how happy he was to have me as a part of the team and then—wait for it—brought out a carrot cake so I would feel at home. I was nearly brought to tears by the kindness.

The act of being invited to the meeting included me, but the gesture to welcome me with something that was meaningful was inclusive practice. How can we create learning environments where everyone feels they belong? Certainly, I am not advocating that we bake desserts for all our learners, but that we get to know them deeply, that we learn about their interests, and that we design instruction with them in mind. It is not enough to invite them into our learning spaces if we cannot also give them what they need so they always hear the message, "You get to be exactly who you are, and you are welcome here."

The Opportunity Myth

During the past decade, the concept of inclusive education has been evolving from simply placing students in general education classrooms to engaging all students in the general education curriculum through whole-school applications, and providing full membership and belonging among age peers (Choi et al., 2018). There is clear evidence about what works for learners, but many students do not yet have access to the resources and support they need to succeed. A study, "The Opportunity Myth" (TNTP, 2018), summarizes the research on the practices necessary for student success.

> Most students—and especially students of color, those from low-income families, those with mild to moderate disabilities, and English language learners—spent the vast majority of their school days missing out on four crucial resources: grade-appropriate assignments, strong instruction, deep engagement, and teachers with high expectations. . . . This lack of access is not random. It's the result of choices adults make at every level of our educational system. We're asking all adults whose choices affect students' experiences to commit to unraveling the opportunity myth.

As leaders, we can unravel the opportunity myth by creating systems and structures that ensure that all students have access to inclusive classrooms that provide them with grade-appropriate assignments, strong instruction, deep engagement, and teachers with high expectations who make students feel as though they truly belong. This is the foundation for our multi-tiered system.

All students, regardless of disability, English language proficiency status, income, race, or academic performance, can receive Tier 1, 2, and 3 services. All students are general education students first, and the focus of MTSS should be creating strong Tier 1 systems and supports. Recent research argues that inclusive education is connected to the movement for effective schools and school improvement, making it clear that what happens in general education classrooms, in terms of organization, interventions, and activities, has a critical impact on the academic success of all students (Arnaiz-Sánchez et al., 2020).

One of our favorite sayings is this: "You can't intervention your way out of weak Tier 1," because Tier 1 general education classrooms provide the foundation for a multi-tiered system. Understanding what effective Tier 1 programming looks like is critical to creating changes necessary to meet the needs of all learners.

Too often, inclusive placement is tangled with inclusive practice, as if physical presence in a room equates to being inclusive. It does not. Inclusive practice includes the removal of barriers concerning participation, achievement, and presence while also using instructional and behavioral strategies that improve academic and social-emotional outcomes for all students, with and without disabilities, in general education settings (Ellery, 2020; Massachusetts Department of Elementary and Secondary Education, 2019).

Inclusive practice is at the heart of equity in schools. Waitoller and Kozleski (2013) defined inclusive practice as a movement that emerged in response to systemic exclusion of students viewed as different (e.g., students with disabilities, ethnically and linguistically diverse students, and students from low socioeconomic backgrounds) from meaningful and equitable access and participation in education.

The United Nations (2020) recently published an article, "Universal, Inclusive Education 'Non-Negotiable'." The article notes, "The core recommmendation of the Global Education Monitoring (GEM) report is to understand that inclusive education means equal access for all learners, notwithstanding identity, background or ability." According to UNICEF (2013) in the State of the World's Children report, "Inclusive education entails providing meaningful learning opportunities to all students within the regular school system. It allows children with and without disabilities to attend the same age-appropriate classes at the local school, with additional, individually tailored supports as needed" (p. 7).

Universal Design for Learning

Universal Design for Learning is a powerful framework to operational-ize the right to education, supporting educators in maximizing desirable challenges and minimizing unnecessary difficulties (International Disability Alliance, 2021). UDL is a framework for designing learning experiences, so students have options for how they learn, what materials they use, and how they demonstrate their learning. When implemented with a lens of equity in a multi-tiered system, the framework has the potential to eliminate opportunity gaps that exclude many learners, especially those who have been historically marginalized. If we want all students to have equal oppor-tunities to learn, we have to be incredibly purposeful, proactive, and flexible (Novak, 2021). UDL creates a learning environment that is the least restric-tive and most culturally responsive and trauma-informed for all students.

Pause and Reflect

What is your familiarity with the Universal Design for Learning (UDL) framework? Differentiated instruction? Consider what you know about the frameworks already, and what questions you have. You can return to these questions at the end of the chapter to determine if your understanding of the frameworks has evolved.

The term "Universal Design" was coined by architect Ronald Mace in 1988 who defined it as the "design of products and environments to be usable by all people, to the greatest extent possible, without the need for adaptation or specialized design" (Center for Universal Design, 1997). Buildings where all people could not enter were deemed "architecturally disabling."

In Mace's (1998) last public speech, he shared more about his philosophy on UD. He said:

> Universal design broadly defines the user. It's a consumer market driven issue. Its focus is not specifically on people with disabilities, but all people. It actually assumes the idea, that everybody has a disability and I feel strongly that that's the case. We all become disabled as we age and lose ability, whether we want to admit it or not. It is negative in our society to say "I am disabled" or "I am old." We tend to discount people who are less than what we popularly consider to be "normal." To be "normal" is to be perfect, capable, competent, and independent. Unfortunately, designers in our society also mistakenly assume that everyone fits this definition of "normal." This just is not the case.

UDL is based on research in cognitive neuroscience that guides the development of flexible learning environments that can accommodate learner variability. UDL is defined by Higher Education Opportunity Act (PL 110-135) as "a scientifically valid framework for guiding educational practice that (a) provides flexibility in the ways information is presented, in the ways students respond or demonstrate knowledge and skills, and in the ways students are engaged; and (b) reduces barriers in instruction, provides appropriate accommodations, supports, and challenges, and maintains high achievement expectations for all students, including students with disabilities." Given that inclusion of students with disabilities in general education settings is contingent on teachers' ability to use inclusive instructional strategies, wide-scale commitment to UDL will be critical in creating multi-tiered systems (Scott, 2018).

Before effectively implementing inclusive practice, we must embrace the concept of variability. As stated in *UDL Theory and Practice*, a book by two of the founders of UDL, "From one perspective, human brains are remarkably similar. But to neuroscientists, this similarity is an illusion" (Meyer, Rose, and Gordon, 2014, p. 29). All learners learn in ways that are unique to them. This is referred to as variability.

We want to caution that embracing student variability is not the same as designing instruction based on learning styles. An article in the *Atlantic*, "The Myth of Learning Styles," shares the pervasiveness of the learning styles myth (Khazan, 2018). More than 90% of educators in various countries believe in their presence and use them to design instruction. But spoiler alert—there is no such thing. This is not to say that we do not have a unique mix of strengths and weaknesses, cognitive variability, multiple intelligences, or preferred learning approaches. But our brains are not wired for a single "style" of learning.

If someone says, "I am a visual learner," or "I need to hear it, to learn it," this idea stemmed from the theory of learning styles. There is just one problem: the theory is not grounded in science. Multiple studies have proven that learning "styles" are no more than learning "preferences" and that a preference doesn't lead to better learning outcomes (Nancekivell, Shah, and Gelman, 2019).

If we cater to a student's "learning style" by giving the "visual learner" more visual information and more aural information to the "auditory learner" or more movement to the "kinetic learner," we will shortchange their learning process. This does not mean we can't embrace multiple forms of intelligence and provide numerous scaffolds and supports. We should provide visual, auditory, linguistic, conceptual, and sociocultural scaffolds, but not because of learning styles—because of variability.

Pause and Reflect

Did you ascribe to the theory of learning styles? If so, notice the cognitive dissonance you may be experiencing as you "unfreeze."

In *UDL Now! A Teacher's Guide to Applying Universal Design for Learning,* third edition (Novak, 2022), variability is unpacked in terms of *interpersonal variability* and *intrapersonal variability*. Certainly, as educators, we know that our learners are very different from each other. This is interpersonal variability. There are still models where "struggling readers" are placed in a different classroom than "advanced readers" because the student needs are different, but this doesn't embrace intrapersonal variability. For example, we may be in an "advanced" reader group. It is likely that our group will not receive options to listen to the audio version of the text or access sentence stems because we "do not need them." But what about days when we are exhausted and having a terrible day, or when we forget to wear our glasses, or when the most responsible thing we could do for our mental health is to take a more accessible pathway to find balance? Instructional groups, when they are used for placement, do not embrace intrapersonal variability. Our needs are always changing.

The lack of appreciation of learner variability, especially intrapersonal variability, causes many learning environments to be restrictive and disabling to students. According to Liz Hartmann, an adjunct lecturer on education at Harvard University and an expert in UDL (2015), "When teachers embrace the conceptual shift of the UDL framework and learner variability, they understand that severe disabilities are part of the natural diversity that is to be expected and embraced in classrooms" (p. 58). When this shift occurs, educators are much more likely to provide the options and choices necessary for students with disabilities to thrive in inclusive classrooms.

Once educators embrace variability, inclusion, and the promise of UDL, they adhere to three principles when planning learning experiences: provide multiple means of engagement, multiple means of representation, and multiple means of action and expression. Considering these principles removes the barriers that make curriculum and instruction "disabling" to learners, especially students with disabilities (Meyer, Rose, and Gordon, 2014):

Provide multiple means of engagement. Student engagement is equal parts attention and commitment. For students to pay attention, they need learning opportunities that are relevant, authentic, and meaningful. Since students are different from one another, and because they are dynamic and their needs evolve based on context, no one lesson will be authentic to everyone. To be committed to authentic learning, students need to learn how to maintain effort and persistence, cope when learning experiences are challenging, and self-reflect to help guide their learning. In a universally designed classroom, these skills are explicitly taught by providing students with opportunities to practice these skills in meaningful ways as they work toward their goals.

Provide multiple means of representation. When teachers present information, they often use a single representation and provide the same lesson to all students. This is often done in a lecture, by playing a video, conducting a lab, or presenting or demonstrating information, teaching vocabulary, and so on. Because there is significant variability in students, they differ in the information they need to gather before applying it in an authentic assessment. By providing multiple opportunities and options for students to learn information, students are empowered to personalize how they build knowledge and skills.

Provide multiple means of action and expression. Once students are interested in authentic learning outcomes and have learned the information by selecting the options that best meet their needs, they need to express their understanding in an authentic assessment. When students participate in discussions and complete assessments, they are taking action and expressing their learning. If we want all students to have equal opportunities to communicate their learning, we need to design flexible pathways. To do this, it is critical to unpack our standards and ask, "How can we design opportunities where all students can share their progress toward the standards?"

The three principles of UDL support educators in creating multiple pathways for students to learn and express what they know while empowering students to make choices about their learning. Although this framework does allow students with disabilities to thrive in their classrooms, it also increases the engagement and achievement of all students (Scott, 2018). Understanding the three principles is the foundation for building learning experiences that work for all students and make effective inclusion possible. The three principles of UDL support educators in providing options and choices so students have pathways for how they engage with learning, learn, and share what they know.

The UDL principles are further broken down into the UDL Guidelines (CAST, 2018), a collection of evidence-based strategies that embrace variability and support expert learning that are continually evolving. As of the publication of this book, CAST's website notes, "Because the UDL Guidelines are meant to be informed by feedback from the field as well as new research, they have been updated several times in the past. We are in the process of updating the Guidelines once again in our UDL Rising to Equity initiative. This update will focus specifically on addressing systemic barriers that result in inequitable learning opportunities and outcomes."

UDL Now! (Novak, 2022) reminds readers, "Know that regardless of the language of the current or future Guidelines, they are just that—guidelines. They are not prescriptive and "one-size-fits-all. Think of the guidelines as a Swiss Army Tool that can be used in many ways." Because UDL and its core principles have evolved with education, it has grown to impact every major education initiative today.

UDL is sometimes confused with differentiated instruction, a complementary but different framework. Whereas UDL is about proactively designing flexible learning environments where students can make choices to self-differentiate their learning, differentiated instruction is an approach where teachers modify curricula, methods, materials, and assessments to address the diverse needs of individual students and small groups of students (Tomlinson et al., 2003).

Given this discussion, the differences may not be obvious. Table 3.1 identifies what makes each of the frameworks unique.

Table 3.1　Components of UDL and differentiated instruction.

UDL	Differentiated Instruction
• UDL is focused on student-centered learning where the learning experiences are proactively designed so options are accessible for every learner. • The goal of UDL is to remove the barriers to learning so students can achieve optimum knowledge and become expert learners. • UDL asks us to design flexible goals, methods, materials, and assessments by considering diverse learner needs from the beginning. • UDL provides multiple means of engagement, representation, and action, and expression to all learners. Students are encouraged to self-differentiate and choose the best path for themselves.	• Differentiated instruction (DI) can be seen as a responsive practice where adjustments are made based on the individual needs of the students and small groups of students. • Often, differentiation is done after the data is collated and trends are noticed. • The goal of differentiation is to provide a responsive and optimal learning environment for individuals/groups of learners. • DI provides targeted strategies that are teacher-directed to support student learning.

Source: Adapted from Choudhury (2021).

The National Center for Learning Disabilities (NCLD, 2021) published a research brief that examines evidence-based approaches to accelerating learning. This brief discusses the importance of UDL and robust multi-tiered systems. They advise:

- Streamline curriculum while focusing on grade-level standards, which connects to UDL's focus on firm goals
- Allow for additional time to integrate necessary prerequisite skills
- Customize instruction based on strengths and areas of growth for each student
- Leverage student interests that lead to deep, engaging learning
- Use Universal Design for Learning (UDL), multiple modalities, and small group instruction

The connections to UDL are explicit, but there are also areas where differentiated instruction (DI) is necessary, specifically when noting that some students need "additional time to integrate necessary prerequisite skills" and using "small group instruction." In inclusive classrooms, teachers use feedback from formative assessments to create groups of students. After reviewing the results of universally designed assessments, you will often find there are three categories of students (McGlynn and Kelly, 2017):

- Students who have fully mastered the content or skill and are ready to move on or access additional challenges
- Students who have a basic understanding of the content and/or skill
- Students who do not yet have an understanding of content and/or skill

In a universally designed classroom, students access firm goals and flexible means but their outcomes are not the same. To accelerate learning, teachers need to create small groups of students based on data to provide additional instruction or support. This is where differentiated instruction comes in.

These frameworks complement each other in a multi-tiered system, but first, best instruction should be designed using the principles of UDL. When evidence suggests that students need additional support, intervention, or enrichment, teachers can differentiate instruction to supplement, not supplant, universally designed learning experiences.

Pause and Reflect

How can UDL and differentiated instruction (DI) complement each other in multi-tiered systems of support (MTSS)? To look at this another way, why is it critical to provide self-differentiated learning and targeted intervention and support in small groups and individually?

Universal Design for Learning (UDL) is often thought of as simply providing choice, as a lesson planning template, or as a framework for curriculum design, but it is much more comprehensive. It is the expression of a belief that all students are capable of learning. When crafted and implemented with this belief, instruction can help all students succeed in inclusive and equitable learning environments. In *UDL Now!* (Novak, 2022), UDL is described in terms of beliefs, skill sets, and systems:

Beliefs. In a universally designed classroom, teachers have to believe that all students can learn at high levels and that inclusive placement is necessary for success. Teachers must also believe that students are capable of becoming expert learners who can make effective decisions for themselves when given conditions of nurture and the opportunity to try. No exceptions.

Strategies and skills. Belief systems are not enough. Educators must continually build a skill set to design with student variability in mind. They have to learn how to unpack learning outcomes and design assessments where students can share what they have learned in relevant, authentic, and meaningful ways. But a UDL skill set is more than lesson design. To eliminate barriers that prevent students from learning, educators must be trauma-informed, culturally responsive, and know how to support students academically, behaviorally, socially, and emotionally.

Systems. To create universally designed classrooms, schools, and districts, educators need district support. District professional development, leadership practices, high-quality and flexible curriculum, available technology, and schedules all impact an educator's ability to meet the needs of all learners. Recognizing system barriers is important as we design action plans to create multi-tiered systems. MTSS plans strategically address these barriers, which ensure that UDL can be scaled and optimized district-wide.

Pause and Reflect

As you consider the barriers that prevent all students from accessing Tier 1 inclusive and equitable instruction with their peers, would you categorize them as barriers to mindset, skill set, or system barriers? Know that all three can be addressed through a comprehensive MTSS.

We have had many leaders and educators ask us for UDL-driven resources focused on what an educator must possess to successfully engage in UDL for students. To look at this another way, what capacities does an educator need to have/be able to do to remove barriers to learning when designing Tier 1 instruction that is inclusive and equitable? Table 3.2 identifies skills necessary to universally design instruction. Consider using Table 3.2 in one of the following ways:

- Share Table 3.2 in an upcoming faculty meeting or professional development session. You can encourage colleagues to use the tool as a self-assessment. Educators can consider areas where they identify relative efficacy as well as areas where they would benefit from collaboration, feedback, and support. We all have areas where we can grow. That is what being an expert learner is all about.
- Use the tool to vet your current professional development offerings. Are you providing ongoing support for all learners to eliminate barriers that may interfere with learning? Is your professional learning focused on designing instruction to meet each learner's needs academically, behaviorally, socially, emotionally, and culturally? If not, how could you begin to share or model strategies as you work as a team to scale inclusive practices in your school or district?
- Use as a tool to inspire mastery-oriented feedback within informal or formal observations. When you identify practices that may create

barriers for learners, share some resources to support educator practice and growth.

Table 3.2   Skill set of a UDL practitioner.

Predictable Barrier	Skills
Students may not be interested in content or may not know why content is important.	• Building meaningful relationships with students to learn more about their interests and needs as learners is critical to ensure there are options that align with their interests and needs. • Given the wealth of diversity in our public schools, culturally responsive pedagogy is necessary to create a comfortable and academically enriching environment for students of all ethnicities, races, beliefs, and creeds. • Ability to articulate essential standards and why they are important.
Students may lack motivation to continue to persist when there is a significant challenge.	• Foster growth mindset in students. • Understand and model self-regulation strategies so all learners have tools to persist when struggling. • Understand what executive function is (attention, working memory, and flexibility) and how to support all learners. • If students are struggling, it is critical to offer them mastery-oriented feedback, or concrete suggestions about how to get back on track. Learn more about providing effective feedback to better support learners.

Table 3.2 (Continued)

Predictable Barrier	Skills
Students may struggle with self-regulation and expected behaviors.	• Understand the functions of behavior. • Implement a robust tiered behavioral system (i.e., PBIS) so there are clear behavioral expectations in every learning environment that are consistently modeled and reinforced. • Facilitate social emotional learning in all aspects of curriculum and teaching. • Be trauma-informed. • Understand restorative practices and how they can minimize threats and distractions for learners.
Students may not be able to comprehend instruction if only a single modality is used (overreliance on lecture, or text, for example).	• Support learners in accessing and using multiple representations of the same information (i.e., podcasts, videos with captions, text). • Provide explicit and direct comprehension instruction.
Students may struggle to comprehend the language or symbols used in the learning environment.	• Provide explicit vocabulary instruction and use visual resources to clarify vocab. • Implement sheltered-English immersion strategies to support English language learners in accessing rigorous content.
Students may struggle to express what they know if given a single modality without adequate scaffolding.	• It is important to universally design assessments to ensure that the assessment is reflective of what the student has learned, rather than being reflective of a barrier they are experiencing. • Understand the three types of scaffolding (linguistic, conceptual, and sociocultural) and how to universally design instruction with the scaffolds embedded.

Pause and Reflect

1. In which areas do you feel that your colleagues have strong efficacy? Why? Discuss the support that was provided to build competency.
2. What is one skill on which you want to focus your attention to better meet the needs of all learners?
3. How does this tool help you integrate multiple focus areas as you focus on UDL and inclusive practice?

UDL can also offer a framework for viewing and calibrating inclusive instruction to help increase teacher efficacy. Building teacher efficacy is the practice of building "teachers' confidence in their ability to promote students' learning" (Hoy, 2000). The team at Novak Educational Consulting (2022) created a UDL look-for document to help teams calibrate their understanding of UDL (see Table A.1 in Appendix A). This tool can be used by teachers, instructional coaches, and evaluators to observe and set goals for more universally designed learning opportunities in the classroom. The tool was designed with a focus on instructional coaching, and instructional coaching questions, because of its documented impact on teacher efficacy. Research is clear that instructional coaching can significantly impact teacher efficacy when the following elements are in place (Javius, 2020):

- Trust with a teacher is developed and leveraged to have honest conversations surrounding the current level of efficacy.
- The coach has to develop an uncanny knack for assessing the "will and skill" of the teacher.
- The coach provides high-quality and timely feedback to the teacher to engender immediate instructional action.
- The coach can cultivate a "psychological safe space" with the teacher to engage in racial equity, if applicable in the coaching relationship.
- The coach solicits feedback on their coaching to examine their efficacy of coaching-up teachers.

Pause and Reflect

How could you and your team use the UDL Look-for Tool in Table A.1 in Appendix A to reflect on, calibrate, and/or improve inclusive instruction so all students can access Tier 1 classrooms with their peers?

Deeper Learning

The book *Equity by Design: Delivering on the Power and Promise of UDL* (Chardin and Novak, 2020) demonstrates the need for deeper learning experiences aligned with UDL. Not only do students need access to classrooms that are engaging and universally designed, but they need those classrooms to celebrate their identity. The section "Where to Begin? Reflecting on Ourselves, Our Students, and Our Systems" notes, "Education today should be designed to elevate and celebrate the voices of students. A focus on teaching advocacy and channeling student passions in our classrooms needs to replace our focus on depositing knowledge to students sitting passively in rows" (p. 6). This is a call for deeper learning experiences for all students.

The Learning Policy Institute defines deeper learning as "teaching and learning practices that enable students to learn core academic content in ways that apply their knowledge to relevant problems" (Hernández and Darling-Hammond, 2019, p. 3). Deeper learning approaches help students think critically and solve meaningful, complex problems using mathematical, scientific, and creative reasoning.

Deeper learning experiences require collaboration, effective communication, and self-directed inquiry, enabling students to "learn how to learn" and develop academic mindsets that increase perseverance and productive learning behaviors (Roc, Ross, and Hernández, 2019). When classrooms are designed with UDL and deeper learning, all students can demonstrate mastery, identity, and creativity, defined below (Mehta and Fine, 2019).

- Mastery is evident when all students develop the knowledge or skills outlined in the standards and practices, with the ability to transfer that knowledge across situations.

- Identity is evident when all students become more invested in the discipline by thinking of themselves as active agents who do that kind of work. To support a shift in thinking from "I'm learning about biology" to "I am a biologist," educators affirm each student's cultural and racial heritage and leverage their funds of knowledge, experiences, and interests.

- Creativity is evident when all students shift from receiving the knowledge of a discipline to acting or making something within the discipline. Students engage with tasks that have multiple paths to multiple standards-aligned solutions.

The book *In Search of Deeper Learning: The Quest to Remake the American High School* (Mehta and Fine, 2019) offers the following explanation of the three virtues:

> In the spaces that teachers, students, and our own observations identified as the most compelling, students had opportunities to develop knowledge and skill (mastery), they came to see their core selves as vitally connected to what they were learning and doing (identity), and they had opportunities to enact their learning by producing something rather than simply receiving and knowledge (creativity). Often these spaces or classrooms were governed by a logic of apprenticeship; students had opportunities to make things under the supervision of faculty and older students who would model the creative steps involved, provide examples of high-quality work, and offer precise feedback (p. 7).

Incorporating deeper learning into your MTSS work is critical to ensure that all students have access to enriched environments where they are challenged and stimulated, and higher-order thinking and performance are expected (Noguera, 2017). Deeper learning draws directly from research on culturally responsive pedagogy, which ensures that diverse students engage in academically rigorous curriculum and learning, feel affirmed in their identities and experiences, and develop the knowledge and skills to engage the world and others critically (Escudero, 2019). Gloria Ladson-Billings (1995) proposed three main components of Culturally

Relevant Pedagogy: a focus on student learning and academic success, developing each student's cultural competence to assist students in developing positive ethnic and social identities, and supporting students' ability to recognize and critique societal inequalities. All three components must be utilized to lead students to academic achievement, cultural competence, and sociopolitical awareness. It is critical to ensure that all students have access to culturally sustaining pedagogy, a theoretical stance proposed by Django Paris (2012) that "seeks to perpetuate and foster—to sustain linguistic, literate, and cultural pluralism as part of the democratic project of schooling" (p. 93).

The integration of this research and the focus on mastery, identity, and creativity in the definition of deeper learning is based on a deep belief that all students can engage in authentic, meaningful, and rigorous learning experiences with their peers. We want to design systems that consider student safety, foster belonging, and support agency (Riley, 2018).

We want to ensure that each student's physical and psychological safety is central to the design of our systems and environments. Here, not only are students' physical safety needs being met, but they feel safe to make mistakes in our classrooms or come to an adult when they need emotional support. When it comes to belonging, we want to make sure that all students feel that they are valued members of our learning community. We also want to promote agency so all students, regardless of identity, feel empowered to play an active role in their learning.

Pause and Reflect

What connections can you make between UDL and deeper learning? Reflect on the classrooms in your school or district. Do all students have access to Tier 1 classrooms where UDL and deeper learning are guaranteed while students work toward grade-level standards?

Deeper Learning Tasks

The Kaleidoscope Collective for Learning, a project of the Massachusetts Department of Elementary and Secondary Education (DESE), provides tools and protocols to support the development of deeper learning experiences.

The Collective defines deeper learning tasks as tasks that have a clear purpose, provide students with diverse perspectives, and require students to create meaningful products. The Collective's definitions of purpose, perspectives, and products, shared below, are particularly insightful, aiding educators in evaluating the efficacy and potential for deeper learning in any given learning experience. The application of these definitions serves as a benchmark for assessing a task's potential for comprehensive and meaningful learning. (Massachusetts Department of Elementary and Secondary Education, 2023b).

Purpose. Students engage in a task that is part of a coherent, standards-aligned curriculum. The task is accessible to all students and engages students in the work of the field or discipline.

Perspectives. Educators and students not only engage with resources from diverse perspectives but also analyze who is centered, who is excluded, what social narratives are preserved, and the purpose for preserving those narratives. This attention to criticality drives educators and students to deepen their thinking skills to better understand the connections between content and societal contexts.

Products. Students create and answer questions, generate hypotheses, gather materials, collaborate with one another, and discover opportunities to apply learning in a meaningful product, and share their ideas and solutions with those directly and/or indirectly impacted by the problem.

As with all evidence-based instructional practices, it is critical to create a multiyear strategy to close the research-to-implementation gap. Just as UDL requires shifts in beliefs, skills, and systems, so does a transition from more traditional models of instruction to deeper learning and traditional assessments to deeper learning tasks. In a report from the Learning Policy Institute, "Deeper Learning Networks: Taking Student-Centered Learning and Equity to Scale" (Hernández and Darling-Hammond, 2019), researchers share four key insights that can inform districts and schools seeking to expand access to deeper learning and equity in a wide range of settings. As you reflect on the implications summarized here, note the relationship to implementation science, improvement science, and what you have learned about MTSS (p. 8):

- School design and pedagogy are intimately linked. Deeper learning pedagogies require other structural changes that reorganize how educators work together, school schedules, high-quality instructional materials, and the development of authentic assessments.

- Every stakeholder must learn about the new approaches and why they matter to make decisions and contributions that sustain these approaches. The research stresses the importance of stakeholder engagement and collaboration. The report notes, "In addition to teachers and school leaders, central office leaders, school board members, teachers' unions, parent and community groups, and local businesses need to understand deeply what new models of practice are seeking to accomplish and how they intend to do it."

- Developing the pedagogies needed to teach for deeper learning with equity requires new approaches to professional learning: one and done professional development will not result in, nor sustain, system change. Districts need to consider how to provide ongoing support for educators in pedagogies, using high-quality instructional materials and designing authentic assessments aligned to grade-level standards. It is also critical that professional learning mirrors deeper learning (Adams and Duncan Grand, 2019).

- School leaders must have significant knowledge of learning and successful experience in the new model to redesign the school and help enable the innovative practices it requires.

To ensure that all students have access to UDL and deeper learning, we have to organize our schools and districts for success. In addition to providing teachers with professional learning to transform Tier 1 instruction, we have to integrate multiple components into a "comprehensive package of school supports comprising school leadership, parent-community tiers, and a student-centered learning climate" (Bryk et al., 2010). The recognition that we need a systems lens to ensure all students have access to inclusive, equitable, authentic deeper learning experiences is why you are reading this book. We are called to create systems and structures so we can guarantee that every child in our district has opportunities to learn at high levels with their peers while engaging in a meaningful and rigorous learning environment. Understanding more about inclusive practice, UDL, and deeper learning can help you to craft a vision for the work ahead to drive your strategy moving forward. As you prepare to craft that vision, take a moment to pause and reflect on the following prompts that will help you to brainstorm a vision for the students you serve that incorporates inclusive practice, UDL and deeper learning.

Pause and Reflect (questions adapted from Chardin and Novak, 2020)

Take time independently or with colleagues to journal your answers or foster courageous conversations using the following questions:

- What is our desired impact?
- Who do we want our students to become?
- What world, society, and/or time period are we preparing them for?
- What does it look, feel, and sound like when we are successful?
- What role do we play in student success?
- How have we engaged in courageous conversations?
- How do we acknowledge and celebrate differences?
- Do all members of our school community feel safe, seen, and heard?
- Does our work validate the lives and experiences of folks from different backgrounds and/or identities?

Summary

The purpose of MTSS is to ensure that all students have equitable access to Tier 1 classrooms that meet their needs academically, behaviorally, socially, and emotionally. Equitable MTSS requires significant shifts in mindsets, skill sets, and how our systems and structures are designed. When leaders are immersed in strategic work to create more comprehensive multi-tiered systems, they have to demystify what it means to have inclusionary practices and inclusionary placements and share the importance of Universal Design for Learning (UDL), and deeper learning as core frameworks in inclusive classrooms.

Reflection Questions

1. At the beginning of the chapter, we asked you to consider what you know about UDL, differentiated instruction and deeper learning and to pose questions about the frameworks. Return to those questions to reflect on if your understanding of the frameworks has evolved.

2. UDL requires schools and systems to focus on beliefs, skills, and systems work. In your experience, which areas are the most challenging to address?

3. What systemic shifts can you make to create conditions, so that deeper learning occurs in all settings?

4. What specific indicators can we monitor in our system to ensure that UDL and deeper learning occurs in all settings?

4

Building Your Team and Crafting a Vision

In this chapter, we focus on an old adage, "Teamwork makes the dream work." As cheesy as that may sound, it is true. A single person cannot support adaptive change at scale. It is critical to assemble a core leadership team to guide MTSS while ensuring that representative stakeholders from advisory teams have opportunities to contribute to strategic planning, monitor progress, and communicate impact. Numerous protocols and tools are provided throughout the chapter to support you in establishing a high-functioning team committed to a shared vision of success for all learners.

The Ultimate Dream Team (Katie)

My kids are obsessed with sports. At dinner, they spend an inordinate amount of time constructing their favorite teams in each sport—all-star lineups in anything from lacrosse to competitive eating. My son Brec recently announced that Joey Chestnut is the greatest athlete of all time because he holds fifteen mustard yellow belt "titles" for his Fourth of July eat-a-thons. We can agree to disagree.

At one point, they asked me who my favorite team was, and I didn't hesitate to answer—the 1992 United States Olympic Basketball team, dubbed the Dream Team. It was the first year NBA players were allowed to play in the Olympics, and all my favorite players came together to make magic. I had a T-shirt, the collector's cereal box, and named the squirrels in my yard Stockton, Ewing, and Barkley!

What made the team so darn impressive wasn't only their incredible talent, but how they worked together. Decades after they dominated the world's stage in basketball, the Bleacher Report (2010) wrote, "The beauty of it was that the way they integrated all their stardom and personalities to create a flawless display of teamwork. Even though they had MJ and Bird, two of the most prolific scorers in NBA history, it was Charles Barkley who led the team in scoring. Coach Chuck Daily never had to call a timeout. The team gelled together even though they were accustomed to competing against one another."

Teamwork Makes the Dream Work

All it takes is one dysfunctional team experience to understand the value of having the right team in place. The work of systemic change is not an easy one. An unnecessary barrier to success is having the wrong team in place to lead this work. It can breed dysfunction and slow the process. In our experience, you have to surround yourself with the correct team members to bring your work and vision to life, just like the Dream Team of the '92 Olympics.

If we are going to make robust systemic change to meet the needs of all learners, we must not hide away with a group of comfortable confidants. Rather, we must share this work with the community we serve and must engage them with diligence. It is possible to gel even with competing views. In fact, it may be a team's greatest strength.

Establishing the MTSS Team

In an effective MTSS system, representative stakeholders with the authority to make district decisions must collaborate with each other as well as with students, staff, families, and community partners. Defined strategies for engagement are essential, such as collaboration protocols, communication plans, feedback loops, stakeholder surveys, targeted outreach efforts, and so on (Durisic and Bunijevac, 2017).

Before you craft your vision, complete your needs assessment, or begin creating your strategy for MTSS, you must build buy-in and engagement within the organization and the greater community. Too often, the work of MTSS is done in a central office or school leadership meetings and is not shared with all stakeholders until the work is complete. We strongly advise against this practice.

The Washington Office of Public Instruction discusses the importance of the MTSS team in their state MTSS framework (Washington Office of Superintendent of Public Instruction, 2020). The guidance notes:

> [MTSS] Leadership teams are responsible for building the capacity of the team to lead the work as well as providing ongoing training and support to staff, families, and community partners to implement as intended. Leadership teams should have broad representation and an established process to regularly solicit input and collect data from staff, students, families, and community partners.

How does one ensure that voices from all students, families, and communities are used to drive improvement efforts? To begin with, representation on committees is a start. We also must focus on outreach efforts and assess existing methods of outreach to see if the voices being spoken and listened to represent the community, with a specific lens to remove barriers to participation (e.g., transportation or language barriers). We must not wait for our stakeholders to ask for materials to be translated but rather be proactive in our efforts to prioritize such services.

If we are going to create a system that represents the lived experiences of our students and their families, we have to commit to elevating historically marginalized voices in the planning and design process. Too often, parents find their names listed among the collaborators on strategic planning documents but feel that they did not participate meaningfully or make a substantive contribution (Graham, Kennedy, and Lynch, 2016).

Team Members On a basketball team, you need people in different positions—point guards, shooting guards, and coaches. Having a balance of players and positions allows the team to function; the same is true with our MTSS work. Systems-level change requires a guiding team to represent the entire organization and encompass various stakeholders and decision-makers. First, you need a coach. District improvement efforts should be led by the superintendent or the primary leader of the organization. We have had too many experiences where key decision-makers are not leading this work. From experience, we can tell you that you do not want to facilitate meetings where everyone looks at each other and says, "Well, we really can't decide this now. Let's make an appointment with the superintendent to see what she thinks."

The Minnesota Department of Education (2021) provides a roadmap that supports districts in creating their core MTSS team. They recommend that the core team consist of leaders responsible for behavioral health, special education, curriculum and instruction, equity and inclusion, technology, business and finance, and research and evaluation as well as a representation of school principals and teachers and the district's superintendent.

Additional stakeholders can serve in advisory roles by offering their perspectives, feedback, and broad recommendations on how to build on the district's strengths and challenges. We recommend you have a core leadership team and an MTSS advisory group with members from numerous stakeholder groups. Their input informs the work of the leadership team charged with developing the improvement plan and provides insight and input throughout the implementation of the plan. Table 4.1 shows examples of members and tasks across multiple planning teams. Of note, you will see a reference to multilingual learners in this section and throughout. We define multilingual learners as students who are linguistically and culturally diverse, and as such enhance our organizations with their assets (WIDA, n.d.).

Pause and Reflect

- Do you already have a core MTSS team? If so, who is on it? Are there any critical stakeholders missing?
- Do you have an MTSS advisory team? If so, who is on it? Are there any critical stakeholders missing?

If you do not have these teams yet, consider why it would be important to create teams that can monitor the progress of your MTSS implementation while also having an advisory group to provide feedback and elevate the perspectives of diverse stakeholders.

Table 4.1 Recommended team configuration.

Team	Representative Membership	Functions
Improvement Planning Leadership Team Members	• Central office: superintendent/executive director, central office staff (e.g., behavioral health, special education, curriculum and instruction, equity and inclusion, technology, business and finance, and research and evaluation) • Building level: principals, assistant principals, curriculum coordinators, coaches, etc.	• Initiatives review • Data review • Document review • Self-assessment • Logic modeling • Planning design • Implementation measures development
MTSS Advisory Team Stakeholder Team Members	• School and district leadership • Staff • School committee • Parent community • Student community • Consider existing advisory groups such as representatives from the school site councils, parent-teacher organizations, special education and multilingual learner parent advisory councils, school and district partners, and student leadership groups. • Other stakeholders may include union representatives, community organizations, statewide assistance team members, or social service organizations.	• Create the vision • Review the findings of the leadership team • Engage in staff, student, and family/ community surveys • Asset mapping • Community-facing survey design • Review and feedback of the plan • Share the plan • Ongoing feedback on implementation

Team Process   A high-functioning and knowledgeable team is essential to lead this work. If your team is collaborating to design a multi-tiered system of support, it is important that they be a well-functioning team and one that understands MTSS. This ensures that the work you engage in is not contingent on any one person who may or may not be there when the plan is fully implemented. We have worked with far too many districts that have to replicate this entire process every time a new superintendent is hired. The MTSS plan does not belong to the superintendent. It belongs to the district. When done well, the plan can continue despite leadership changes.

We always recommend that you take the time to immerse your core MTSS team in ongoing professional learning. Read your state MTSS guidance, have discussions about your current MTSS systems, and collaborate to complete MTSS self-assessments so everyone on the team understands the work ahead and is committed to seeing it continue.

The amount of active meeting and workshop time is important. Ask yourself: Are our meetings frequent enough to make an impact? Some stages of planning will require more sessions than others. For example, when conducting a needs assessment, the MTSS advisory team may meet monthly, but individual members may need to host numerous focus groups and data analysis sessions in between the meetings with their stakeholder groups. The frequency of meetings and between-meeting commitments (what we affectionately call "what happens between the boxes") should be provided to team members in advance.

This work takes time, so at the beginning of the school year, schedule meetings for the year so you have time set aside for this critical work. When we worked together as superintendent and assistant superintendent, our core leadership team met for a half-day twice a month to focus on MTSS and our ongoing improvement efforts. We would schedule additional meetings if we needed more time to complete projects like a document review or data analysis, which we will discuss in detail later in the text. Examples of these activities/timelines are shown in Figure 4.1 within an average school year.

Building Team Norms   One of the first things the team should do is make sure everyone understands the work of the team and what their roles are within the group. This is important within your core leadership team

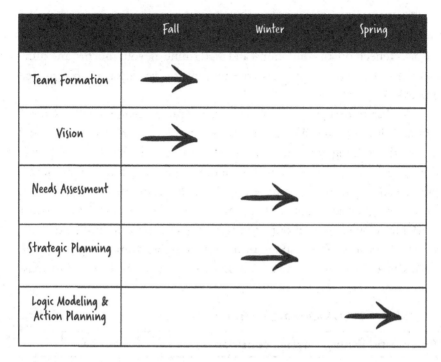

	Fall	Winter	Spring
Team Formation	→		
Vision	→		
Needs Assessment		→	
Strategic Planning		→	
Logic Modeling & Action Planning			→

Figure 4.1 Timeline of activities for core MTSS team.

and when working with your MTSS advisory group. Outlining the expectations for the members and their level of decision-making is key. Another great opening activity is to have members engage in self-reflection to harness their personal "why" for participating in this work.

It is a good idea to establish norms from the onset to establish a healthy culture during this work and to ensure that stakeholders with diverse perspectives have opportunities to share their voices (Rantung and Sarmita, 2020). Norms are important because they help groups improve teamwork skills that eventually contribute to the effectiveness of the group. We have both worked with numerous teams who feel that the process of creating norms is a little silly, but believe us, without them, people are not on the same page. For example, one person in your meeting can think it is perfectly acceptable to check phone messages during meetings while others do not. This will lead to unnecessary tension, which will impact group dynamics.

In *Keys to Successful Meetings* (Hirsh, Delehant, and Sparks, 1994), the authors pose considerations for creating group norms. If you have norms already, reflect on the questions and determine if your norms are sufficient. Alternatively, you may use the prompts to develop team norms (see Table 4.2).

The key to designing norms is to expand them beyond meeting expectations. It is important to create norms that consider more than starting and ending times. Long gone are reliance on norms that are limited to expectations like "come on time" and "no sidebar conversations." Rather, norms provide an opportunity to create conditions for courageous conversations, for fostering collaboration and community and for designing systems that work for everyone within our organization. This approach must be done in an open and accessible manner. In order to support team engagement, the norms must be representative of those in the meetings. The norms must

Table 4.2   Developing norms.

When establishing norms, consider	
Time	• When do we meet? • Will we set a beginning and ending time? • Will we start and end on time?
Listening	• How will we encourage listening? • How will we discourage interrupting?
Confidentiality	• Will the meetings be open? • Will what we say in the meeting be held in confidence? • What can be said after the meeting?
Decision-Making	• How will we make decisions? • Are we an advisory or a decision-making body? • Will we reach decisions by consensus? • How will we deal with conflicts?
Participation	• How will we encourage everyone's participation? • Will we have an attendance policy?
Expectations	• What do we expect from members? • Are there requirements for participation?

Source: Adapted from Hirsh et al, 1994.

be grounded in culturally sustaining practices and a lens toward removing barriers for active participation by all. As you work with your team, use the following questions to reflect on if your team is culturally responsive and whether it embraces the lived experiences of all members of the team. Having a culturally responsive team will help to drive strategic plans that will result in improved learning for students who have been marginalized from the academic and social curricula of our school systems. To reflect on the cultural responsiveness of your team, consider the following questions (Farmer, Hauk, and Neumann, 2005):

- Does your team validate the life-worlds, identities, and needs of all members?
- Does your team explicitly recognize the value and discussion of how cultural and personal identities mediate the design of curriculum, instruction, and assessments?
- Does your team support the development of awareness among members in knowledge, skills, and value sets associated with access to power?

Pause and Reflect

How would you answer the previous questions? Consider bringing the questions to an upcoming team meeting to grapple with courageous conversations about the identities of all members and access to power and shared responsibility in MTSS work.

To model UDL, we encourage teams to also build and/or revise norms with the framework in mind. Table 4.3 includes questions you can use with your team that are drawn from the UDL Guidelines (CAST, 2018). The answers can be adapted into team norms. For example, when we asked a team, "What must we do to foster collaboration and community," the team realized that they had to be purposeful about setting up their meetings and subcommittee meetings in a way that honored this commitment. They created the following norm as a result: "We will foster collaboration and community by creating flexible options for collaboration in the meeting and with the creation of subcommittees, by creating topic related small collaborative groups, where each group will articulate the group's members, roles, and goals."

Table 4.3   UDL to guide norms.

Provide Multiple Means of Engagement	Provide Multiple Means of Representation	Provide Multiple Means of Action and Expression
What must we do to optimize individual choice and autonomy?	What must we do to offer ways of customizing the display of information?	What must we do to vary the methods for response and navigation?
What must we do to optimize relevance, value, and authenticity?	What must we do to offer alternatives to visual information and auditory information?	What must we do to optimize access to tools and assistive technologies?
What must we do to minimize threats and distractions?	What must we do to clarify vocabulary and jargon?	What must we do to use multiple tools for construction and composition?
What must we do to heighten the salience of goals and objectives?	What must we do to promote understanding across languages?	What must we do to guide appropriate goal-setting?
What must we do to foster collaboration and community?	What must we do to illustrate through multiple media?	What must we do to support planning and strategy development?
What must we do to increase mastery-oriented feedback?	What must we do to activate or supply background knowledge?	What must we do to support planning and strategy development?
What must we do to develop self-assessment and reflection?	What must we do to guide information processing and visualization?	What must we do to enhance capacity for monitoring progress?

Pause and Reflect

- If you already have team norms, review them through the lens of Table 4.3. Do you have norms that address all the questions?
- If you do not have team norms yet, consider bringing Table 4.3 to an upcoming meeting to have a discussion about potential norms.

Coordinating with Other Teams

To assume full responsibility for the outcomes of all students, it is key to coordinate your work with other vital teams. The following is a sample of teams that you should coordinate with. It is not all-inclusive and will vary by the existing or any new teams the organization is forming. We encourage regular communication with these teams and perhaps representative participants from them on the MTSS advisory team.

Leadership Team: All members of the district leadership team inclusive of central office and building-level leaders.

School Improvement Teams (e.g., school councils or Instructional Leadership Team (ILT): These teams can work to design school improvement goals that align with the district plan. This supports the diffusion of the district plan in a contextual way for each specific building.

Grade-Level Data Teams/PLCs: These teams are essential in unpacking grade-level, programmatic, and individual student needs and reviewing data in response to particular instruction and curriculum. The results of their review should inform the district team, and a process should be in place to share patterns and trends across these teams' data with the district team. Team goals at this level should support district goals but apply them in context to the grade level or department.

Student Support Teams: These teams help define tiered supports and interventions for individual students (based on data), so the work your team is doing to design systems of support should interact with these teams. For example, efforts to establish entrance criteria for services should align with a vision of proactive support.

Collective Bargaining Team: If any planning implications impact a collectively bargained agreement, ongoing negotiation and collaboration with this committee are essential.

Professional Development Committee: This committee can help align the professional learning options with the results from the needs assessment and associated action plan to support MTSS.

Parent Councils and Organizations: These teams will provide a two-way communication mechanism with the parent community.

Student Councils: These councils will provide a two-way communication mechanism with the student community.

Understanding Effective Instructional Practice

One of the biggest challenges in instructional vision work is a misalignment in our collective understanding of effective instruction. In the potential absence of this within your organization, we have created a list of effective instructional practices that can serve as this collective definition, as shown in Table 4.4. These are the practices that we would like to see in all classrooms at all times. The table includes a crosswalk of the effective instructional practices against the deeper learning context described earlier in the book. Note how teams can use the *Skillset of a UDL practitioner* in Table 3.2 to help to build their understanding of Universal Design for Learning.

Pause and Reflect

- Consider the classrooms in your school or district. To what extent does each classroom include the elements of effective instructional practice? How do you know?
- Is there one element that is a relative strength? If so, which one?
- Are there elements that the district needs to prioritize to ensure all learners have opportunities to access inclusive and equitable learning spaces?

Table 4.4 Elements of effective instructional practice.

Mastery is evident when all students develop the knowledge and/or skills outlined in the standards and practices, with the ability to transfer that knowledge across situations.	**Creativity** is evident when all students shift from receiving knowledge of a discipline to acting or applying their learning to share ideas, solutions, and/or make something within the discipline.
	Identity is evident when all students become more invested in the discipline by thinking of and seeing themselves as capable and active agents who do that kind of work.
Universal Design for Learning (UDL) helps instructors use multiple means of representation to give learners various ways of developing knowledge and/or skills outlined in the standards.	**Universal Design for Learning (UDL)** uses multiple means of engagement to tap into learners' interests, challenge them appropriately, and motivate them to learn to support student ownership in their own learning.
	Universal Design for Learning (UDL) provides multiple means of action and expression to provide learners with options for demonstrating knowledge and skills by applying their learning to share ideas, solutions, and/or make something within the discipline.
Evidence-based practices result in positive student outcomes for the cohort of students outlined in the standards and the ability to transfer that knowledge across situations.	**Culturally sustaining pedagogy** uses asset-based pedagogical research to inform the design of schools as places where the cultural ways of the students are incorporated meaningfully into the work so students feel connected, capable, and represented in their learning.

(Continued)

Table 4.4 (Continued)

Mastery is evident when all students develop the knowledge and/or skills outlined in the standards and practices, with the ability to transfer that knowledge across situations.	**Identity is evident when all students become more invested in the discipline by thinking of and seeing themselves as capable and active agents who do that kind of work.**	**Creativity is evident when all students shift from receiving knowledge of a discipline to acting or applying their learning to share ideas, solutions, and/or make something within the discipline.**
Standards-based instruction ensures that the instruction is aligned to appropriate grade-level and content-specific state standards.	**Linguistically supportive practices** provide multilingual learners with equitable access to meaningful and rigorous learning opportunities that build on their cultural and linguistic assets as a means to see themselves as capable and active agents in their own learning.	
High-Quality Instructional Materials (HQIM) ensure that the materials used are aligned to state standards and exhibit a coherent sequence of target skills, instructional practices, and understandings.	**Trauma-informed practices** fully integrate knowledge about trauma and use effective strategies that remove barriers presented by trauma as a means of access to robust learning opportunities within the disciplinary content of each classroom.	

Creating the Vision

Once you have your core team and your MTSS advisory team and your meetings outlined for the year, it's time to get cooking! Your team must lead their work via a strong, meaningful vision. The visioning process offers the opportunity to engage a diverse range of stakeholders in the school/district's planning work and ensure that many voices are heard. Diverse perspectives in the planning process will strengthen the quality and effectiveness of the resulting plan, and inviting participation in the planning process will build ownership and advocacy for the resulting plan among both educators and the community. An inclusive approach will also contribute to a positive school/district culture, helping to build a shared understanding of the work required to serve all students as well as the relationships and trust among stakeholders that will support that work.

We worked with a district in a coastal town in Massachusetts. Resisting the temptation to jump straight into MTSS "nuts and bolts," the district's new superintendent and district leaders spent almost two years working collaboratively to craft a new district vision statement and theory of action that would power up school improvement efforts. The superintendent's first move was to listen, learn, and get a feel for the district. The district team was committed to implementing MTSS, but they were concerned about buy-in. Because academics had been part of schooling forever, leaders felt tiered supports and a focus on academics would be familiar for staff. However, SEL was still new. While it speaks to commonsense ideas (learning is fundamentally social-emotional; kids develop social-emotional skills just as they do academic skills), implementation options are many and varied. The MTSS leadership team knew that implementation in uncharted waters, without strategic alignment and focus, can result in a lot of boats knocking into each other at night and a lot of kids without boats. They needed to create a common vision to guide improvement efforts.

The superintendent engaged the MTSS Team to revise the existing vision, using the protocols shared in the next section. She then presented the draft to the school committee and asked members: Is this what we want for our kids? Is this how we want to see the work take hold? The school committee adopted the vision, and this vision and corresponding theory of action has guided district improvement work since and helped staff focus on institutional practices that are obstacles to moving the theory of action forward.

Although it may seem like an incredible investment in time, creating the vision and establishing buy-in is critical for the work. We have to work with diverse stakeholders to create vision statements that center around the success of our students grounded in functioning systems. As an example, reflect on this sample vision statement:

> All students thrive in school, graduate with the skills and knowledge necessary to succeed in the college and/or career of their choice, and contribute to the vivid life in a global community. Each day in our schools, students achieve mastery of grade-level knowledge and skills, experiential learning that matters to them and reflects their identity, and connect content to the social context. We do this by ensuring academic achievement, cultural competence, and sociopolitical awareness. All students, inclusive of multilingual learners and students with disabilities, are immersed in grade-level work that is interactive, relevant, and real-world while engaging in an environment where they feel safe and hold a sense of belonging, agency, and value.

Drafting the Vision

If your organization has an existing vision statement, how well does it align with the concepts of MTSS, UDL, and deeper learning? If fully aligned, go with that! If not, you can revise it or write a new one. The vision statement communicates an ideal result, a vision. It reflects values and beliefs about how students learn best and should inspire and challenge. A vision statement does not describe what an organization currently does nor how your school operates. Rather, a vision statement details an ideal result, a state of being that the school/district would like to achieve. The following is another example of a vision statement. What do you notice about this statement? What values are present?

> Students are curious, engaged learners who are gaining the tools and knowledge to become culturally responsive, positive, contributing members of local and global communities. We have a universally designed,

personalized, flexible, inclusive, tiered instructional model that includes a rich, rigorous, comprehensive, and aligned curriculum measured by authentic assessments. We employ strong professionals who are enabled by continuous training and support to make decisions based on expertise, data, and research. The schools are physically and emotionally safe spaces.

You can use the following steps if you do not have a protocol for developing a vision. These steps serve as a simple approach to this work.

1. As a whole group, determine the timeframe for the vision. Is this where you want to be in 5 years, 10 years, and so on? Next, break into teams of two to three people each and write a draft for the ultimate vision of a school/district that meets the needs of all learners.

2. Coming back together as a group, small groups will share their initial vision statements and will combine these into one vision statement. You may type on a shared doc, project the draft on a screen, or use chart paper. Continue combining vision statements until you have a statement that reflects the consensus of the group.

3. As you review your vision, consider the following and revise as necessary:
   - Does the vision help to create a shared understanding of high-quality instruction, which promotes deeper learning for all students?
   - Does the instructional vision communicate high expectations and advance equitable outcomes for all learners?
   - Does the vision center around the student experience and create conditions for student engagement and agency in their learning?

4. Discuss/plan for how you might engage a wider group of stakeholders (i.e., the MTSS advisory group) and other district teams in the review/revision of your vision statement.

5. Brainstorm ways to share the vision with the community once it is finalized (e.g., a one-pager to distribute, adding the vision to existing documents, creating a video or visual, etc.).

A shared vision supports organizations in considering how their work provides or fails to provide all students with an equitable learning experience rooted in deeper learning, including traditionally underserved students,

students of color, students with disabilities, and multilingual learners. To shift the student experience, the experience of educators in schools must shift as well. This concept is referred to as "organizational symmetry": the mindset, social awareness, and skills we seek to instill in students must be mirrored in the work required of educators, building administrators, and systems leaders. Consider whether that is embedded into your vision as well.

Pause and Reflect

Do you have a district vision? If you are not sure, explore your district web page or reach out to the superintendent. If you have one, reflect on the vision as it relates to MTSS, inclusive practice, UDL, and deeper learning. If you do not have a vision yet, what would be a next step toward working with your community to create one to guide your strategic work moving forward?

Summary

District improvement efforts for MTSS begin with creating a high-functioning core team and an MTSS advisory team that is inclusive and represents the diversity of the organization. Once the team is formed, it is critical to create norms for the ongoing work and establish a vision to guide the work moving forward. Using the vision as a North Star for improvement efforts will be key to meeting the needs of all students.

Reflection Questions

1. What plans do you have to make sure that your MTSS advisory team is both inclusive and diverse with representative stakeholders throughout the district community?
2. Why is it critical to create team norms that address time, listening, confidentiality, decision-making, participation, and expectations?
3. How will you create and share your vision for MTSS and inclusive practice?

5 | Kicking Off the Needs Assessment Process

In this chapter, we walk you through a process that will help you build an understanding of your current systems and their impact on all learners so you can begin to identify what needs to change. This starts with reviewing current strategic initiatives, a document review process, asset mapping, and completing a systems inventory. Each step in this process will help you to better understand your current system so you can compare it with your vision for a system that better meets the needs of all stakeholders as they engage in authentic, deeper learning experiences.

My Reflection in the Mirror (Kristan)

There is not much that makes many of us feel more vulnerable than looking in the mirror. As I land head first in midlife, I often frown when I catch my reflection. In my head, I still feel like I am in my twenties, but my body betrays this idealized vision. My slumped posture reflects my sore knee and back, my gut is more prominent than in years past, and I see the wrinkles framing my eyes. Yet, as I near 50 years of age, I have begun to appreciate these features. My knee aches partially because it helped me climb the Himalayas, my back hurts as a result of many years of dancing, my waist is thick because of the privilege of eating island cuisine daily, and my wrinkles are a reflection of the many laughs I have had with loved ones and many days spent under the sun. This appreciation does not mean I should not address the things I see in the mirror.

To be healthy and live longer, I need to take care of myself. I need to start walking more to ease my knee pain, I need to stretch more and have a better posture to lessen my backaches, I need to be consistent with my Zumba and pickleball routine to stay in shape, and I need to apply more moisturizer and sunblock to help heal my skin. As I see my flaws, I both appreciate them and address them. Similarly, in our schools, we must look in the mirror. This process should be one of reflection, appreciation, and inquiry. It must help us create the path toward improvement by understanding where we currently stand. It must be an accurate reflection.

Where Do I Start? (Katie)

I have always been a long-distance runner. There is something so peaceful about being the first one up, pulling on sneakers, plugging in earbuds, and hitting the pavement. I first got hooked on running in freshman year of high school, and from then, I didn't stop until I got pregnant with twins. I know that many people run when they are pregnant, but I just didn't do it. And so in the nine months of carrying my babies, I got woefully out of shape. A couple of months postpartum, I dreaded running again. I knew it would be hard because I hadn't run in over a year. It seemed like too much work to get back to running 20 miles at a time. Walking a mile to start seemed pointless. Why start if that's all I can do? Spoiler alert: You have to start there.

So often, district and school leaders think about everything they have to accomplish and it is so difficult to know where to start. We are staring down the proverbial 20 miles of frameworks and initiatives. There is so much to do: create multi-tiered systems of support, implement UDL, become more culturally responsive and trauma-informed, learn how to facilitate blended, remote, hybrid, and concurrent learning. It is so overwhelming that we feel maybe it's just easier to wait until there is a better time to start. That is a trap. Don't do it. Now is the time to start. But where can you begin?

Seeing Our Current Systems

Let's roll up our sleeves and get started. You have a team and you have a vision, but that won't be enough. If anything is true about the past couple of years, it is that the inequities of our systems have demanded our collective attention. This is not to say that individuals have not spent their lives working to dismantle these systems, but discussing equity and access wasn't always a dinner table conversation in every home. And now it is.

When writing strategic plans, schools and districts often start by reviewing the vision, or the "why" of the work. Nearly every vision we have read embraces success for all learners. The key word is "all." This is critical but it's not enough to have a vision. Our vision statements, which strive for success for all, are out of reach if we continue to design systems and instruction the way we have always designed them. We cannot serve all students until we design learning that embraces the brilliance and lived experiences and identities of our Black and Brown students, learners with disabilities, multilingual learners, students who are economically disadvantaged, LGBTQ students, students who experience trauma, and students who need more social, emotional, behavioral, or academic support than we currently provide.

As you have learned from previous chapters, facilitating meaningful and sustainable systems-level change related to MTSS is a complex process. It requires an understanding of the components associated with the evidence-base for MTSS, effective implementation practices, and a system-wide approach (Eagle et al., 2015). An effective districtwide MTSS needs assessment guides action toward systems-level change on many levels, focusing on multiple drivers.

It is time to review your current system to determine areas of strength as well as areas of need. It is helpful to begin by reflecting on your current initiatives to determine if they are serving your journey toward your vision. In every school and district in the world, there are numerous initiatives or things the system is doing focused on improving some aspect of how the schools function. Strategic initiatives are the projects and programs that support and will achieve your strategic objectives. We recommend reviewing all current initiatives with your core MTSS leadership team. Resources and staff energy can only be stretched so far. It is important to consider existing initiatives and how inclusive practice work aligns to meet the needs of your students. You can use the activity in Table 5.1 to guide this work.

Table 5.1   Reviewing Initiatives.

Step	Process
Brainstorming (10 minutes)	• Ask participants to brainstorm all the initiatives they think are happening in the district. If you are meeting in person, you can write these initiatives on sticky notes. If you are meeting virtually, you can create a shared document or a Padlet to brainstorm. • Once all initiatives are posted, the group can review them and eliminate duplicates.
Sorting (10 minutes)	• Review the initiatives to see if there are any that people are unfamiliar with. If so, ask other group members to explain each initiative. • Participants will group the initiatives into themes/categories. The team can choose the kind of category they want. For example, are they under big headers like "Competency Drivers" or broken down into smaller categories such as recruiting and PD/coaching.

Table 5.1   (Continued)

Step	Process
Assessing the Initiatives for "Fit" (40 minutes). Note: Depending upon the number of existing initiatives, this protocol may take longer.	Once the categories are firmed up, place initiatives under these categories. The following list is a series of questions. Discuss your answers as a group. Ensure that one member of the team records this discussion. For each initiative, answer the following prompts: • Is this "initiative" already ingrained in the work and no longer needs to be a focus of change? • Is there an understanding of this initiative, what it is, who is involved in it, who is leading it, etc.? • Has this initiative had positive outcomes for students? If so, how do you know? • Is it high lift and low leverage (or the reverse)? In other words, is there a lot of time and energy spent on this initiative but not a large impact being felt for all that work? • Does this initiative meet the language and spirit of your vision statement? In other words, if you continue to do this work, will it support or undermine your vision? Please remember that some initiatives are mandated and you will need to plan for their integration even if they do not align perfectly with your district vision. Based on the results of this discussion, you may have difficult decisions to make. For example, you may need to decide if you should continue an initiative. If so, the following should be considered: • Is your team able to make this change? If not, who else should participate in the conversation? • If you decide to change/stop an ongoing initiative, what is the consequence/impact of that? • How will you communicate these changes to impacted stakeholders?

Source: Adapted from Curtis et al (2009).

Document Review

Once your team has identified your current initiatives, it is time to complete a document review to better understand the current strengths and needs of the district. To best understand the lived instructional design in your system, it must be evidenced in tangible artifacts of practice. There are a number of documents that your district can review as an initial form of self-assessment. Your process should never "create" resources but rather reflect on those that exist already. In this process, you not only collect them but engage with them. As you collect and examine your documents, ask yourselves the following questions:

- What story do they tell?
- Is each document aligned with your current vision?
- Is each document supporting a robust tiered system of support?

Table 5.2 provides a sample of important documents to review as you reflect on your current systems and structures. We do not suggest you review all documents but choose those that align with your vision and your current systems or lack thereof.

Once you identify the documents you want to review, you must have a discussion about the implications of this review. During this process, the team reviews the documents through the lens of MTSS. The review team must have an existing understanding of MTSS and use this to assess their current practices.

Pause and Reflect

Review Table 5.2 as a checklist. Consider which of the documents you have already and which you would need to collect to facilitate a comprehensive document review to drive an MTSS needs assessment. The following considerations may be helpful:

- Who will review the documents? Will the core MTSS review all the documents or divide them among small groups?
- How will you share the document review process with the MTSS advisory group and other district groups for feedback?
- How will this document review process help you to better understand district strengths and needs as it relates to building comprehensive MTSS?

Table 5.2 Sample Document Sources.

Core Documents	Additional Documents
• Strategic Plan, District Improvement Plan, and School Improvement Plans	• Human resources office procedures manual and any other associated materials, particularly those articulating recruitment, hiring, or placement procedures
• Most recent budget proposal with any narrative/presentation used and approved budget for past three years	
	• Description of the curriculum review process (e.g., identification, piloting, adoption)
• External audits (i.e., equity, financial)	• Student, faculty, and family handbooks, including codes of conduct
• Curriculum pacing guides, scope and sequences, and sample curriculum documents or curriculum units	• Internal and external evaluations of mandated programs (such as multilingual learners, special education, and Title I) and of other programs and services (such as needs assessments, community partnerships, and curriculum reviews)
• Assessment maps	
• Summary of existing curriculum materials	
• Documents that describe or illustrate structures, policies, or practices related to data analysis and use (e.g., description of the district data team; protocols used for data analysis at the district, school, or classroom levels)	• Most recent accreditation report
	• Documents that describe or illustrate the way in which the district assesses school climate and conditions for learning within the school
• Description of tiered supports provided to students who are not meeting benchmark	• Guidance for schools about how to engage with families; information about opportunities for family leadership (e.g., Special Education Advisory Council, School Advisory Council)
• Description of Tiers 1, 2, and 3 academic, behavioral, and social emotional supports for all students	
• Sample IEPs and 504's	
• Classroom observation protocols or look-fors	• High school course enrollment and course passing data
• High school program of studies	

(Continued)

Table 5.2   (Continued)

Core Documents	Additional Documents
• Forms, documents, observation tools, and templates used in educator evaluation system for all educators, such as rubrics, educator plans, and observation and evidence gathering forms • Documents that describe or illustrate district- and school-based student support teams or similar teams that meet regularly to discuss student academic, social emotional, and behavioral needs • Professional Development (PD) Plan and description of current PD program, along with documents or data illustrating evaluation of PD, including curriculum-specific professional development plans for all grades • Documents that describe or illustrate the district's efforts to recruit and retain a diverse workforce and build the cultural competency of its staff	• Copies of data analyses or reports used in schools, such as analyses of student performance on midterm and final examinations and benchmark and formative assessments • Examples of ways in which the district shares student performance data with students and families • Documents that describe/illustrate educator recognition, leadership development, and advancement program(s) and opportunities • Description of induction and mentoring program and/or associated handbook/materials • Teacher common planning time schedules • Sample agendas from relevant team meetings and schedules for the year (e.g., leadership team meetings, common planning time meetings)

Source: Adapted from Massachusetts Department of Elementary and Secondary Education (2022).

As an example, imagine the MTSS team reviews the master schedule of a high school in the district as well as individual teacher schedules. When scheduling for a tiered system of instruction it is recommended that there be dedicated intervention, and/or enrichment blocks for all students that are provided by qualified personnel, including classroom teachers and special educators, Title 1 educators, English language learner educators, and the like. For students in need of additional support in a targeted area, the intervention block is an opportunity to review, relearn, and master the skills in that area. For students who have demonstrated proficiency in the curriculum being taught in their classrooms, or who need an additional level of challenge, the enrichment block provides an opportunity to develop a deeper understanding of key concepts and to apply and integrate learning from core content. Additionally, schedules in multi-tiered systems need adequate time for common planning. Planning time helps improve instruction by allowing teachers to share best practices, examine data, discuss students' work, engage in instructional related PD, and plan curriculum and lessons together. In order for common planning to contribute meaningfully to student outcomes, sufficient time should be built into the schedule.

There are numerous barriers that prevent the development of master schedules that provide adequate time for tiered scheduling for students as well as common planning for educators. Hanover Research (2014) argues that the most common challenges include building consensus among stakeholders and ensuring adequate common planning and professional development time for educators to prepare to meet the needs of all learners.

In the review process of examining the high school schedule, the team recognized that the schedule did not allow authentic tiered support to be available to all students, nor did it offer common planning for all educators. The following section summarizes the document review of the high school schedule review. It does not represent the full scope of the document review; rather it is intended to demonstrate the framing of how the team viewed the high school schedule in relation to building robust tiered systems of support. The necessary schema needed for this activity was an understanding of MTSS schedules.

Document Review Sample: High School Schedule

Before completing the document review, all members of the core leadership team reviewed the state MTSS guidance to build a shared understanding of the components necessary to build an inclusive and equitable system. They understood that in order to build a strong MTSS, their schedules had to prioritize and allocate time to support all educators and students and include adequate time for core instruction, assessments, intervention time, team meetings, and planning. The team used a set of criteria from this guidance to form their review lens. The following are the components of their schedule that they assessed:

- Did the schedule support student achievement and equity, providing supplemental support for students academically, behaviorally, socially, and emotionally when they need it?
- Did the schedule ensure that all students have access to Tier 1 inclusive instruction as well as access to advanced coursework?
- Did the schedule allow students to move seamlessly into and out of Tiers 2 and 3 interventions/supports, as appropriate?
- Did the schedule support teacher common planning time, collaboration, and consultation?

For each question, they reviewed effective practices. When examining the question "Did the schedule support teacher common planning time, collaboration, and consultation?" they engaged in a dialogue about the implications of the question. As they reviewed individual teacher schedules and the master schedule, they reflected on and discussed the following questions:

- Do all educators have sufficient time for shared planning?
- If there is common planning, what types of activities occur during these meetings?
- How is common planning time supported to ensure it is implemented well and rigorously?

To help answer those questions, they used tools such as the following guidance from the National Center on Time and Learning (2014). They assessed whether the schedule provided the following:

- 60 min/week for grade-level meetings (minimum)
- 60 min/week for data analysis (minimum)
- Opportunities for regular content level team meetings
- Partner staff to regularly participate in teacher meetings discussing student progress
- Student support services staff to regularly participate in teacher meetings discussing student progress

- Specialty/elective teachers to regularly participate in teacher meetings discussing student progress
- Opportunities for additional informal/non-mandatory grade-level meetings during common planning/prep time
- Opportunities for additional informal/non-mandatory content level meetings during common planning/prep time
- Additional collaboration time beyond regularly scheduled meetings, such as peer-observations, coaching, full faculty PD, and so on

Table 5.3 includes their notes as a result of their document review, research, and discussion. After reviewing Table 5.3, you may be thinking, "How on earth is our team going to complete this process?" Worry not—we have felt that too, but the investment in the needs assessment process is critical to building a shared understanding of needs and identifying objectives for strategic improvement. An effective districtwide MTSS needs assessment guides action toward systems-level change on many levels, focusing on multiple drivers. Think of each element you examine as a potential cog in the machine that will ultimately support all students. This *is* the work.

Asset Mapping

Selecting staff, identifying sources for training and coaching, providing initial training for staff, finding or establishing performance assessment tools, locating office space, assuring access to materials and equipment, and so on are among the resources that need to be in place before the work can be done effectively (Fixsen et al., 2005; Saldana and Chamberlain, 2012).

In a guide for resource mapping in school districts from the University of Maryland (Lever et al., 2014), the authors note that it is common for schools and districts to lose track of the resources they have available for all learners. They note common reasons for this lack of mapping:

- With everyone being so busy, school staff has not taken the time to share the resources that they are aware of with one another.
- Many times the decision to use a given resource was made related to a particular funding stream, mandate, or as a reaction to a particular incident rather than as part of a systematic mapping process.

Table 5.3 Team document review of master schedule.

Review	Documents	Review Notes
Current Schedules	Master Schedule and 10 Teacher Schedules	**Tiered Scheduling** • The schedules do not allow time for evidence-based instruction and interventions to be delivered across all three tiers in order to meet the academic, social, emotional, and behavioral needs of students. • The schedules also do not allow for time to administer assessments to determine the specific needs of all students.
		Common Planning Time • The schedules do not offer consistent and equitable department, grade, and student-level team collaboration and critical follow-up activities • Common planning time is not inclusive of interventionists, special educators, ESL teachers, and student support staff • There are no specified times allotted for staff to analyze assessment data and determine the appropriate supports for each student.
		Inclusive and Equitable Resources • The budget does not include a focus or narrative that speaks to a prioritization of tiered instruction with the flexibility of movement within the tiers. • There is not presently enough staff available to provide tiered support in this schedule. • There is no intervention time built into the schedule.

- Awareness of a given program may be limited to a school or a small subset of individuals within a school, even when services may be available to the larger community.

Over time, it becomes easy to lose track of all the supports and resources that are available, who can access them, how they can be accessed, and the reasons that they are offered. SWIFT Education Center (2017) provides a process for a comprehensive examination of existing resources to help schools consider possible reallocation of resources to best support all students within an MTSS framework:

1. Asset-mapping: Develop an inventory of all currently available resources in the school and district such as personnel, facilities, and curriculum.
2. Once a school maps out currently available resources, they may consider how to allocate time as well as the personnel and facilities listed in the asset map.
3. Lay out a timeline for all resource allocation in the district. When is the budget developed? When does hiring happen? When are grant proposals written? When will the next district strategic plan be written? When does professional development happen?
4. Identify sources of data that you'll have for monitoring the effectiveness of your implementation and adjusting the course as necessary.
5. If necessary, lay out implementation over several years, perhaps three to five, to allow for more gradual reallocation of resources. Stage the implementation so staff can get comfortable with it and become effective step by step.

The process of resource allocation begins with resource mapping. Resource mapping is a system-building process historically utilized by communities, organizations, schools, and service centers to align resources, strategies, and outcomes available (Crane and Mooney, 2005). *Resource Mapping in Schools and School Districts: A Resource Guide* (Lever et al., 2014) provides a framework for this process. Examine the following questions as you map out available resources:

- What do you want to map? While it can be helpful to have a resource directory that includes a broad array of resources and programs, it is also important to be realistic about whether your team can identify and maintain a directory that extends beyond the school building. Use these reflection questions to help guide the process. What kind of resources do you want to map (e.g., assessments, curriculum, personnel)? Do you want to know what is available in the school building, or do you want to know what is available within the community?

- What is the scope of your mapping project? If you include community resources that are available outside of the school building, how broadly are you reaching out (e.g., neighborhood, community, district, state, national)?
- What other guidelines do you want to place on your team's mapping process?
- What format will you use to record the assets/resources? What will your map look like?
- How will you share this work?
- Who will have access to entering/updating the data?
- Where will the database be housed?
- Who will have access to the final product?

Pause and Reflect

Has your district or school facilitated an asset-mapping process to guide the MTSS strategy?

- If so, review the asset map through the lens of the questions in the previous section.
- If you have not yet completed an asset-mapping process, share the process with your team and note its importance for future strategic planning.

Systems Inventory

Drafting a systems grid is a great place to map your assets. Here you look at how the systems are supported with real data from your schedule and staffing models. It is broken into group size, time of support, support duration, associated staffing, materials, and assessments (see Table 5.4). Of note, we want to pause and say that in a true MTSS, all students, regardless of disability designation or IEP status, should have access to Tier 3 if their assessment data indicates the need.

You can start the process by completing a template (see Table 5.5) where you identify your current systems. These systems are those that are currently and broadly in place. In other words, these cannot be reflections of isolated examples. But rather, if we were to come in unannounced, would we see these across all schools and classrooms? You can choose to conduct this system's inventory for specific domains, levels, and subject areas.

Next, you may want to use the same template (Table 5.5) to articulate ideal systems. These are the systems you are working to implement in the future. At this point, do not allow current limitations to impact the development of your ideal system. Rather, we want these to be the kinds of systems we would design if we could be free to make changes without any barriers. Similarly, you can conduct this inventory for specific domains, levels, and subject areas.

Summary

Completing a thorough needs assessment process is critical to building inclusive and equitable MTSS. Too often, the process of reviewing initiatives, document review, and asset-mapping is rushed, which impacts buy-in and transparency and potentially results in strategic plans that do not address the most critical drivers. Taking time to complete each of these components with your core leadership team is necessary but not sufficient. After completing this phase, share the results of this process with your wider MTSS advisory team and additional teams you identified in the explore phase.

Table 5.4   Sample of tiered systems grid.

Tier	Group Size	Time	Duration	Staffing	Materials	Assessment
Tier 1	Full class 25+ students	50 minutes/daily	All year	Co-taught/general ed, and special ed	High-quality curriculum	3x/year universal screener/benchmark assessment
Tier 2A	5–8	50 minutes/daily (WIN)	Quarter cycles	Classroom teacher	Curriculum-based intervention components	Curriculum-based measures
Tier 2B	3–5 students	50 minutes 3–5 days/week	Quarter cycles	Interventionist (Title 1 reading teacher)	Evidence-based intervention	Diagnostic and biweekly progress monitoring
Tier 3	1–3 students	50 minutes/daily	Semester cycles	Reading specialist/special educator	Specially designed instructional materials	Diagnostic and weekly progress monitoring

Table 5.5   MTSS systems template.

Tier	Group Size	Time	Duration	Staffing	Materials	Assessment
Tier 1						
Tier 2A						
Tier 2B						
Tier 3						

Reflection Questions

1. How close are we to our vision, based on our current systems?
2. How can the initiatives review, document review, and asset-mapping process inform our understanding of where we presently stand within a tiered system of support?
3. How might we capitalize on our existing assets as you work toward our vision?
4. What data and systems do you anticipate need to be shifted based on your inventory of existing practices?

6 | Data Analysis to Prepare for MTSS

In this chapter, we focus on creating robust data systems that allow you to monitor progress toward your vision. We focus on the importance of triangulating four types of data including outcomes data, instructional data, perspectives data, and systems data. Additionally, we recommend looking at all forms of data through an equity review to recognize the impact of your current systems on learners who have been historically excluded, marginalized, and minoritized. We also offer concrete guidance and planning tools to prepare your data culture so that you can create rapid cycles of improvement.

The Power of Lived Experiences (Kristan)

I have a memory as a child of my sister being carried away on a small inflatable mat, deep into the ocean waves. I am not even sure if it is an imagined or a true memory, but this is what my brain remembers.

It was a calm day in West Africa, and the waves were not menacing. Our family looked away for just a minute, and when we looked back she was waving her arms in fear as her little plastic floatie carried her deeper into the sea at a pace that frightened us all. My father was a strong swimmer. I remember him swimming with the power of a father's adrenaline to save his child. He snatched her back, and through the large waves, they rolled and kicked to shore. At that moment, we felt only relief.

Later, my parents would establish much more defined ground rules for the use of floatation devices in the ocean. Chiefly, they were to be used in the lagoons but never in the open ocean. What was leisurely in one setting was literally life-threatening in a different environment. Had we had access to the internet in the early '80s, we might have looked up the conditions of the sea and undertow in that location or researched the safety of this float in that setting. Had we been experts in engineering, we could have calculated the risk scientifically and mathematically. We did not have access to that information then, but the lived experience and experiential outcome were all the data needed to change our practice.

Data Analysis

Thus far, we have discussed the importance of reviewing current initiatives, completing a thorough document review, and mapping our current resources and assets. As a next step, you will dive into data (hooray!). When used correctly, data is a tool that helps us to reflect on the outcomes of our actions. Data brings us back to Newton's Third Law of Motion: For every action, there is an equal and opposite reaction. In the world of MTSS, we argue that for every action, there is data to reflect on the reaction.

Although it may not win us popularity contests, we strongly believe that data is a driving force in making your organization work for all students. When data is not examined, or worse, when it is used incorrectly, it can also be a shield to cover areas where we are not positively impacting all learners. Unearthing data, disaggregating it to examine the impact of our actions on all learners, and sharing what we learn is the first step in creating an organization centered on meeting the needs of all of our students, not just some of our students.

Yes, yes, we know that students are more than just numbers. We are in full agreement. Data is more than numbers. We have to examine qualitative and quantitative data from multiple sources to better understand the experience of the learners and families we serve, especially those historically underserved and excluded from the best our systems offer.

The data review process can be overwhelming, so we like to think about collecting data in four categories: outcomes, instructional, perspectives, and systems (see Figure 6.1) (Massachusetts Department of Elementary and Secondary Education, Commonwealth Consulting & Novak Education, 2022, p.4–5). It is important to note that while school and district processes may vary, it is crucial to leverage the perspectives of diverse stakeholders and consistently ask, "How do we know?" to anchor data on the student experience. In many cases, we must not wait until we get all of the most aligned assessments to begin to use data to enhance our tiered supports. Rather, we use what we have and engage in our data tree development.

Pause and Reflect

Before we dive into data, reflect on your current beliefs about data and how data is used in your school or district to drive improvement efforts. What is one word you would use to sum up your personal beliefs about data? Your district data culture?

Outcomes Data

Looking at student outcomes, including accountability data, can provide a high-level view of progress toward your vision and where there may be gaps in opportunities for particular students (such as in specific grade levels, subject areas, schools, or student populations). These outcome data can help you identify more targeted instructional data for a closer look at student experience in the classroom, including examining curricular materials and observing instructional strategies. Together, these data sources can help point school systems toward areas worth exploring in more detail as potential focus areas for continuous improvement. Student outcomes data may include the following, disaggregated by specific student groups:

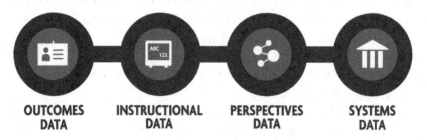

OUTCOMES   INSTRUCTIONAL   PERSPECTIVES   SYSTEMS
DATA   DATA   DATA   DATA

Figure 6.1   Four categories of data

- State accountability data
- Additional measures of student achievement (screening assessments, benchmark assessments, formative assessments, performance assessments, portfolios, student work)
- Student attendance, dismissal, and discipline rates
- Course enrollment, completion, and pass/fail rates, including enrollment in advanced coursework
- Student promotion, graduation rates, and drop-out rates

As you examine student outcomes data, find a way to summarize this data to begin to tell your organization's story. The data points shared represent your priorities. The "Sample Data Summary: Student Outcomes" on the next page is a sample of student outcomes data from a high school. The school is using existing assessments while they look to form their assessment committee to look at different universal screening measures and diagnostic assessments. Based on this data summary, what do you think their priorities are?

Pause and Reflect

As you reflect on the data summary, what do you believe are the school/ district priorities?

Instructional Data

This is data that represents the lived experiences of our students. Observing classroom instruction and reflecting on the curriculum resources shared with students is critical in multi-tiered systems, and this must extend beyond formal educator evaluation. It is the kind of data that informs our thinking about the system's ability to meet the instructional vision that we have set. Sample data sources may include, but are not limited to:

- Observation data such as learning walks, instructional rounds, and evaluation data
- Use of high-quality instructional materials (e.g., lesson plans, student tasks or assignments, and appropriate scaffolds)

Sample Data Summary: Student Outcomes

The school was found to be making "Moderate progress towards targets (25%)" and was "Not requiring assistance or intervention" This represents a carryover of prior year results and an increase over the previous year, which was "23%, Partially meeting targets." In the most recent accountability report, Student Growth Percentages (SGP) are below the state average in both ELA and math across all cohort groups. Students with disabilities have a lower rate of access to advanced coursework (58.7% to 65.7%) but a higher grade 9 passing than their peers in the state (92% to 83.7%).

Based on the FY20 enrollment, an analysis was conducted on the two largest percentages of district enrollment: Hispanic (83.3%) and White (14.1%).

- The percentage of Hispanic students with access to advanced coursework was below state averages.
- In 2020, SAT mean scores for Hispanic and White students were below the state's average scores. There is a discrepancy statewide and in the school between the overall performance of Hispanic and White students. The discrepancy, however, is larger at the state level. For example, in the state average, the difference in the mean math score was 76 points versus 46 in this district.

The high school has been identified as having an overrepresentation of a racial/ethnic group in special education as identified by a risk ratio. Currently, 71.25% of the special education population participates in full inclusion.

- Results of instructional materials against a Culturally Responsive Curriculum Scorecard

Perspectives Data

School systems should use the data analysis process to speak directly to students and other stakeholders (including staff members and families) about their perspectives and experiences. Prioritizing the students with the least access to the system's vision will provide a critical perspective on what areas should be focused on for continuous improvement while helping the district center equity in its improvement efforts. Sample data sources may include:

- Stakeholder perspectives (students, families, staff/faculty, community partners) from surveys and focus groups
- Teacher attendance, retention, and churn, as well as any information from exit interviews or other perspectives on teacher culture and morale
- Local culture and climate survey data

Systems Data

Finally, system leaders can use the information unearthed in the data analysis and conversations with students and other stakeholders to identify particular systems and structures closely linked to the focus areas identified for improvement efforts. At this time, you will integrate your work from your document review process to better understand how all the components of the system fit together and impact student outcomes. In addition to the documents you previously reviewed, you may review additional system-specific documentation such as policy handbooks, equity reviews, or staffing plans to understand where these systems are or are not being leveraged effectively. Sample data sources may include:

- Internal or external reviews such as an equity or a staffing review
- Improvement plans (Strategic Plans, Capital Plans, Tech Plans, district or school improvement plans)
- List of vendors and partners providing services (e.g., professional development and student programming)
- Policy, practice, and procedural artifacts (e.g., policy manuals, schedules, handbooks)

Equity Reviews

Whether you conduct an equity review internally or with the assistance of an outside provider, it is essential that you consider a robust approach. The goal of an equity review is to assess student access to high-quality programs, high-quality teaching, just discipline procedures, equitable resources, and root-cause analysis of persistent opportunity gaps for students who have been historically marginalized. According to the National Equity Project (2022), equity is defined as reducing the predictability of who succeeds and who fails, interrupting inequitable practices that impact students, and cultivating the unique gifts, interests, and talents of every student. They note, "When we focus on equity, we expand our community's notions of who belongs, and who schooling is intended to work for, to include and care for everyone. By respecting and bridging our differences in ways that help us heal from harm, we can ensure that every child is seen, valued, and thrives."

The National Equity Project reframes the work of districts, from approaching equity as closing achievement and opportunity gaps, to one developing systems to increase capacity to bring about more equitable outcomes and experiences. Learning for Justice (n.d) (formally Teaching Tolerance), a resource center funded by the Southern Poverty Law Center, "highly recommends" the equity audit resources available through the Mid-Atlantic Equity Consortium (MAEC). The Mid-Atlantic Equity Consortium (MAEC, n.d.) defines an equity review as "an equity audit specifically look[ing] at policies, programs, and practice that directly or indirectly impact students or staff relative to their race, ethnicity, gender, national origin, color, disability, age, sexual orientation, gender identity, religion, or other socioculturally significant factors."

Equity reviews can be extensive or narrow in scope. The following key questions frame the review and provide an inquiry-based approach to understanding programmatic and resource equity for a district's students. As you complete your data review and needs assessment, consider the following questions from a publication from the Alliance for Resource Equity (n.d.), "Ten Dimensions: Resource Equity Diagnostic for Districts." Through these questions and the corresponding framework offered through the Alliance for Resource Equity (n.d.), the goal of the review is to build a "data story" around equity.

- Does the district have a specific policy, mission, and vision regarding educational equity?
- Does each student have access to high-quality and culturally sustaining curriculum and instructional materials?

- Does each student have access to teaching practices that are engaging, culturally relevant, and standards-aligned?
- Do the teacher and the leadership workforce reflect student diversity?
- Does the district's funding system distribute adequate funding based on student needs and enable flexible use of funds in ways that are clearly understood?
- Does each student who needs more high-quality instructional time receive it?
- Does each student experience a safe school with transparent, culturally sensitive, and consistent expectations and discipline policies?
- Does each student have access to effective social emotional learning opportunities?
- Does each student who needs targeted social emotional and/or behavioral support receive it?
- Is each student enrolled in a school and attending classes that are racially/ethnically and socioeconomically diverse?
- Does each student attend a school that actively and meaningfully engages families?

A sample process for an equity review involves an analysis of student data (e.g., performance, attendance, course enrollment, graduation/dropout data, attendance, discipline) to explore trends. Additionally, documents can be reviewed with a lens toward equity. These documents include policies, handbooks, curriculum, professional development offerings, and budgets, similar to the process of reviewing documents for the MTSS document review. Student, family, and staff surveys are examined for patterns and trends with the aim of understanding perceptions and lived experiences. Survey data is complemented with focus group experiences with students, families/caregivers, and staff. The focus group process is a listening session where participants are invited to engage in a group conversation that focuses on three main questions. The following is a sample set of student-facing questions created by the Education Law Clinic of Harvard Law School and the Trauma and Learning Policy Initiative of Massachusetts Advocates for Children (2019):

1. What does your school currently do to help you do well?
2. Is there anything that you need to do well at school that you are not getting?
3. What does a class that you learn a lot in look like, sound like, and feel like?

As your district continually reflects on its strategic work, it will be important to engage all stakeholders by conducting focus groups and listening sessions. The American Institutes for Research (AIR) (2018) under the U.S. Department of Education published guidance for Equitable Family Engagement. They argue that districts need to offer structures for regular listening sessions with families. Additionally, they note the importance of involving community liaisons that capitalize on the value of community members that speak the language and are of the same culture.

By engaging in regular listening sessions, the district can capitalize on the interim success and modify strategies as needed. To conclude, the AIR (2018) document shares, "Schools and districts can successfully make family engagement more equitable and effective by implementing strategies that reflect the needs and values of the community. These strategies may need to be modified as community needs change over time, especially considering that community demographics and culture can change rapidly" (p.13).

When supporting multilingual learners and their families, family-school collaboration involves three facets for success: (1) developing parent involvement programs that are carried out in the home language, are sustained over time, and are responsive to the cultural experiences of the families; (2) understanding the out-of-school experiences of children and how these may differ from the skills demonstrated at school; and (3) providing accommodations for parents of ELs to enhance the effectiveness of parent involvement activities.

It is also critical to involve your governing body in the equity review work. The following narrative is adapted from an actual equity audit review that involved a school board. It is only a small portion of an audit and may not be aligned with your organization's structure but provides a window into the implications of an equity review on district systems.

Transforming Equity Reviews Into Action

The National School Board Association (NSBA, n.d.) encourages school committees to define equity in inclusive terms. Through its own journey, NSBA adopted the following definition of equity:

> We affirm in our actions that each student can, will, and shall learn. We recognize that based on factors including but not limited to disability, race, ethnicity, and socio-economic status, students are often deprived of equitable educational opportunities. Educational equity is the intentional allocation of resources, instruction, and opportunities according to need, requiring that discriminatory practices, prejudices, and beliefs be identified and eradicated.

NSBA recognizes the critical role school committees have in accomplishing equitable outcomes for all students. School committees establish systemwide goals, adopt policy and budgets, and review and provide feedback on school improvement plans, school handbooks, and curriculum. Through each of these areas, school committees are uniquely positioned to reaffirm their commitment to equitable outcomes and to take specific actions to ensure each child thrives in the district's schools.

One of the districts we worked with shared the following goals as a result of their equity review:

1. **Establish an explicit vision and definition of equity.** The school committee can establish its vision for equity by working with stakeholders to explicitly define the concept for the district.
2. **Include the school committee's vision for equity in the school committee policy manual.** The school committee may wish to add a specific policy (AD) within Section A: Foundations and Basic Commitments.
3. **Create a policy specific to equity.** The policy may provide the school board with an explicitly stated focus on educational equity, including the inclusion of equity practices in the district's strategic plan. A sample policy is shown in "Educational Equity."

EDUCATIONAL EQUITY

The school committee's goal is to address the needs of every student in each of our schools. Educational equity for the purpose of this policy is defined as providing all students the high-quality instruction and support they need to reach and exceed a common standard.

To achieve educational equity the district will commit to:

1. Systematically, when appropriate, use district-wide and individual school-level data, disaggregated by race/ethnicity, gender/gender identity, national origin, language, special education, socioeconomic status, and mobility to inform district decision-making.
2. Raise the achievement of all students.
3. Graduate all students ready to succeed in a diverse local, national, and global community.

In order to reach the goal of educational equity for every student, the district shall:

1. Provide every student with access to high-quality instruction, curriculum, support, and other educational resources.
2. Seek to promote educational equity as a priority in professional development.
3. Endeavor to foster and promote a welcoming and inclusive culture and environment within our schools.
4. Provide multiple pathways to success in order to meet the needs of the diverse student body and actively encourage, support, and expect high academic achievement for each student.

The superintendent shall include equity practices in the district's strategic plan and goal strategies to implement this policy. The superintendent, upon request, will periodically report to the committee the progress of the implementation of this policy.

Pause and Reflect

Note how the equity review impacted the district's governing body. Consider the following questions as you continue with your MTSS process:

- What is the impact of making clear connections between your district equity work and the development of a MTSS?
- Why is it critical to involve the school committee in your improvement work to create an inclusive and equitable MTSS?
- How would the school committee policy shown in "Educational Equity" impact your own district's work in creating an MTSS to support all students?

Prepare Your Data Culture

You have documents and data and fingers crossed, and the support of your governing body. Now what do you do with all of it? Alas, it is time to use data to make decisions about school and district improvement. Data-based decision-making is when teams of educators use formative and summative evaluation procedures to make decisions about student intervention/instruction. Throughout your improvement process, your MTSS team will engage in a strategic problem-solving process to identify student needs and designate intervention and progress monitoring protocols. The district and school leadership teams will also use this data to evaluate districtwide and schoolwide outcomes, consider how to make programmatic and instructional decisions based on those outcomes, and use this data to inform the MTSS action plan. We have four concrete tips for supporting data-based decision-making in equitable MTSS:

- Set a positive data culture
- Create a comprehensive assessment map
- Design a data decision flowchart to inform tiered supports
- Create data systems

Set a Positive Data Culture

It is essential that a culture exists that supports the use of data not solely for needs assessment purposes, but to drive instructional decisions and address inequities. Staff can articulate the value of using aggregated and disaggregated data to support all students, and professional development time is dedicated to helping staff learn how to use data to drive instruction and monitor interventions. We created the following prompts for MTSS teams to reflect on data culture:

- What are your current feelings about how this district uses data to impact instruction and improvement efforts? Please be candid in your response.
- What specific steps would we need to take to make data conversations more meaningful in our ongoing work?
- What barriers do we face if we want all stakeholders to have important conversations about data and how that data impacts instruction and improvement efforts?

The conversations that result from the previous questions may impact team norms or future planning. Although it may seem unnecessary to have these discussions, we strongly recommend that you take the time to build a coherent understanding of your data culture. As a leader, you may feel as though there is a strong culture of data, but staff and families may feel differently. Consider the following possible planning implications.

- You may want to collaboratively define a vision for data use in your organization.
- You may want to provide direct professional development on the value of data and on data literacy.
- You may want to assess your organization's capacity for data culture and competency and create a related initiative or action plan item on your improvement plan based on your self-assessment results.

Create a Comprehensive Assessment Map

An assessment map is an inventory of assessments. An assessment map should include universal screeners, diagnostic assessments, and progress monitoring tools focused on academic skill development as well as social emotional and behavioral development across all three tiers. It is critical to reflect on the assessments available to educators so you can identify potential gaps.

Universal screeners identify students who may experience lower than expected academic outcomes and/or need acceleration and enrichment. Diagnostic assessments are administered to students who fall below a pre-determined level in the screening assessment to provide in-depth information about an individual student's particular strengths and needs for Tier 2 supplemental instruction and/or Tier 3 intensive intervention. Progress monitoring assessments are used to assess targeted intervention skills and to mark student progress over time. A sample assessment map for elementary literacy is in Table 6.1 and a sample assessment map for high school literacy is in Table 6.2. You may want to begin with an assessment inventory to identify any gaps. If you recognize gaps in your assessment structure, you will address this when drafting your strategic objectives. Questions to ask at this stage include:

Table 6.1   Sample elementary literacy assessment map.

Tier 1 Assessments Universal Screeners	Tier 2 Assessments Diagnostic Assessments/Progress Monitoring Tools	Tier 3 Assessments Diagnostic Assessments/Progress Monitoring Tools
• iReady	• CTOPP2	• WADE
• mCLASS	• Informal Reading Inventory	• WIST/WIS
• Heggerty Phonemic Awareness	• Elementary Spelling Inventory (ESI)	• Wilson Assessments
• Quick Phonics Screener (QPS)	• Primary Spelling Inventory (PSI)	
• WrAP, the Writing Assessment Program	• Reading Plus	
• Dyslexia Screener	• Phonics Inventory	
	• Word list reading (e.g., Dolch, Fry, curriculum sight word lists)	

Table 6.2   Sample high school ELA assessment map.

Universal Screeners	• (Tier 1) Ohio State Assessments • (Tier 1) STAR Assessments • (Tier 1) StudySync Readiness Screener • (Tier 1) StudySync Benchmark Assessments
Diagnostic Assessments	• (Tier 2) StudySync Placement and Diagnostic Assessment • (Tier 2) Quick Phonics Screener: QPS • (Tier 2) Spelling Inventory Words their Way • (Tier 2) IXL Diagnostic Assessment • (Tier 2) Lexia Placement Screener (Word Study, Grammar and Comprehension) • (Tier 2) TOWRE-2 Two subtests: Sight Word Efficiency (SWE) and Phonetic Decoding Efficiency (PDE). • (Tier 3) CTOPP Comprehensive Test of Phonological Processing. Currently, the best for evaluating phonological processing skills, which must be assessed because these are the challenges that underlie the struggles with reading and spelling. • (Tier 3) The WIAT-4 Dyslexia Index: Grades 4–12+ includes three subtests: Word Reading, Orthographic Fluency, and Pseudoword Decoding.
Progress Monitoring Assessments	• (Tier 2) IXL Continuous Diagnostic Assessment (20 minutes weekly) • (Tier 2) Quick & Easy High School Reading Assessments • (Tier 3) Wilson Reading System or Orton-Gillingham. Progress monitoring weekly or biweekly with diagnostic assessment as needed.

- Do you have to acquire evidence-based universal screening tools, diagnostic assessments, and progress monitoring tools to create a data culture?
- Are the assessment maps consistent across the system within grades?

- Are assessment maps reviewed regularly to ensure they provide effective data to support students across all tiers and domains (i.e., social emotional and behavioral in addition to academic)?
- Do the assessment maps align to assessment calendars that articulate the audience, scope, and timing for each assessment?
- Are pertinent staff trained in assessment protocols and analysis for all adopted assessments articulated on the map?

Design a Data Decision Flowchart

In a multi-tiered system of support, Tier 1 academic, social emotional, and behavioral expectations are articulated and known by all. Within Tier 1 there is a range of supports to meet the needs of all learners. In addition, there is a range of Tier 2 and 3 academic interventions (supplemental to Tier 1) targeted to specific skills/needs of the student and identified by assessment data. All instruction, interventions, and supports are evidence-based, culturally sustaining, and universally designed. Data is used to monitor the effectiveness of interventions regularly.

When you consider the need for assessments to drive the services provided to students, creating a decision-making flowchart or what we call a data tree may be helpful. Too often, we work with schools that do not have clear entry and exit criteria for tiered support. Working with your core team and other stakeholders to create a data tree (Figure 6.2) will help educators decide which students may need additional support.

Create Data Systems

In a well-articulated approach, district and school-level data systems track student performance over time. These data systems provide regular performance feedback to school teams, coaches, and individual staff for problem-solving, professional development, and action planning. Data systems include not only the data sets/platforms but also the meeting times and protocols needed to utilize the data effectively.

The Data Wise Improvement Process, created by Harvard University, is an eight-step model that guides teams of educators from schools or systems in working collaboratively to improve teaching and learning through evidence-based analysis (Boudett, City, and Murnane, 2013). As school

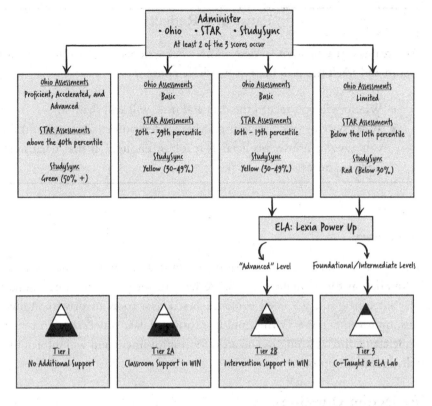

Figure 6.2   Sample data tree

leaders, we are reminded by the Data Wise process that we can help our schools and district decide in advance what short-, medium-, and long-term data we will gather and how we will gather it for future data meetings, and where we will continually loop back to determine the impact we have on all learners. Questions to ask at this stage include:

- Do we have the data systems/platforms we need to track student performance over time and across multiple measures effectively?
- Do all staff have appropriate access to the data they need?
- Do our data systems effectively "talk to one another" and give us a holistic picture of student strengths and needs?
- Does the system set aside time and have defined protocols to ensure data meetings run effectively?
- Is there time to effectively use data to identify student needs and progress indicators via common planning time?

Pause and Reflect

As a team, you will want to determine what systems you have in place to record and track the data metrics you have chosen.

- Where will you record the data and how will you share it?
- What systems (such as your existing student information system) do you have to house this data? Is it robust enough? If not, what next steps are necessary?

Summary

Diving deeply into data, and creating a robust data culture, is necessary as a foundation for equitable MTSS. We have to set goals for more equitable outcomes, and we need evidence-based data tools to drive continuous improvement. Reviewing multiple forms of data is necessary to better understand district strengths and areas for improvement and will inform the self-assessment process.

Reflection Questions

1. How would you describe your current data culture on your team and districtwide? How do you know?
2. Assessment maps are critical to driving continuous improvement. As you consider your suite of assessments, what are the strengths, and where are potential gaps?
3. How does your district currently make decisions about student support based on data? Do you have a data decision flowchart or data tree to support this work? If so, how could the development of one help to support educators with their decision-making?
4. What would you need to change in your school or district to have a robust data system inclusive of a strong data culture, evidence-based assessments, educators who are proficient at using data to drive instruction, time to analyze data, and adequate resources to address areas of need?

7

Conducting
the Self-Assessment

In this chapter, we outline self-assessment as a core component of your MTSS needs assessment process. We recommend working with your core MTSS team to complete the self-assessment using the tools shared in this chapter. The self-assessment aligns with a vision for deeper learning for all students. Once you complete the self-assessment process, we provide guidance to support you in sharing your key findings with all district stakeholders.

Refinishing the Glider (Katie)

Growing up, my parents had a wooden glider that sat on the back patio. I read all my Babysitters Club books while swinging back and forth on that glider. In high school, my best friend, Robyn, and I would stay up late, drinking hot chocolate by the fire pit and looking at the stars from that glider. Fast-forward 20 years, and the glider was headed to the same firepit. "You can't throw away the glider," I told my dad.

He looked at me quizzically; the glider was clearly on its last leg. There it sat, covered in moss and splinters, the hinges rusted and a few boards missing. "I will refinish it," I announced with absolutely no idea how I would do that. I rushed into the project with little thought, and to be honest, it probably took me hundreds of hours and dollars more to complete it than if I took the time to assess the process, create a plan, and acquire the needed tools.

"No need to plan," I told myself, I can just refinish it! Spoiler alert: I did not. At nearly every step in the process, I realized that I wasn't clear on what I actually needed in the first place. I didn't have all the right tools, the right hardware, or let's face it, the right skills. If I could go back in time, I would've sat with my dad and done a comprehensive "Save the Glider Needs Assessment."

If that sounds familiar, it is because it probably is. We work in schools and districts where the needs are clear and we want to jump in and fix them. After you review the documents and data, you may feel like I did with the glider. You're ready to start! But believe me, it's important to better understand the entire process and all the components you will need before you begin.

Now, you're probably wondering, did I save that glider? Yes, I did. But it involved the purchase of many new tools, a gorgeous cobalt blue paint, weeks of my summer, and yes, a couple of visits from my dad. Hey, you can't do this alone, right?

Completing the Self-Assessment

We do not want you to jump into an action plan without taking the time to complete a self-assessment as a means of understanding the scope of the work in order for you to define action steps and your high-priority areas. We must examine our current systems to move closer to a vision of deeper learning for all students.

We created this self-assessment in collaboration with the Massachusetts Department of Elementary and Secondary Education as a way to support planning teams as they identify potential areas of systems design that are in place or need to be put into place. A digital version of this self-assessment is publicly available at www.doe.mass.edu/csdp/guidebook (Massachusetts Department of Elementary and Secondary Education, 2023a). This process is designed to help district teams assess the systems and structures that they have in place already and those they do not have yet, to foster an effective MTSS. This process was designed to give a district-level perspective and should be used by a team consisting of a range of stakeholders. The self-assessment covers many complex elements that you likely will not be able to evaluate easily or immediately. As you preview the self-assessment, consider which data sources and documents you will draw on to respond accurately and thoroughly to each indicator. Generally, when working with districts, we recommend a sequenced planning option or an intensive self-assessment retreat.

For the sequenced planning option, the team meets before conducting the self-assessment to triangulate and analyze data. The team may be the district leadership team or a subset of the larger MTSS advisory group. Prior to completing the self-assessment, the team completes the document review and the data analysis. This can occur in a prolonged workshop setting or over multiple meetings. They then bring this information to the full planning team's self-assessment session(s).

Alternatively, in the retreat option, the team meets in one lengthy session or a series of sequential meetings to analyze data and complete the self-assessment. For this to be effective, the people who need to pull up data and documents are present and available to gather this information during the meeting. Be sure to bring lots of coffee and sweet treats if you're opting for a retreat!

Whatever the format and purpose, we recommend that the self-assessment be data-informed and reflective. For each component, consider a rating scale and have a place to record the narrative. Consider the information you gathered from your document and data review to define your rating. If you have something mostly or fully in place, link in an artifact (document or data) to demonstrate this.

The following is a sample of a rating scale you can use in your self-assessment:

- (0) Not yet in place
- (1) Partially in place
- (2) Mostly in place
- (3) Fully in place

Using the previous rating scale, the following is a sample of notes taken at a self-assessment workshop:

Components	Rating	How do we know?
Vision: The learning community has a shared understanding of high-quality instruction, which promotes deeper learning for all students.	1	• We have a vision, but it is not robustly aligned with all of the effective instructional practices. • We do not have an articulated instructional guide to define what our vision should look like in all settings. • We do not have a fidelity measure to assess if our vision is being enacted in all settings.

You can complete the self-assessment as a team or complete it individually or in small groups and then calibrate the responses. Regardless of how you complete the process, it is critical that the MTSS team requests evidence to justify tool ratings to bolster the validity of the information collected and support consistency in the criteria used (Schiller et al., 2020). If you choose to complete it individually or in small groups first, you may use or adapt the following process:

1. Rating sharing: One at a time, teams share their score for each of the rubric categories—without explanation—as the recorder completes the group's score sheet. For example: "For Vision, our group rated the three items 1, 1, and 2." The recorder would write the ratings in a single copy.
   a. The recorder will highlight any row where there are differences in ratings. Those items will be discussed in the next step.
2. Discussion
   a. The facilitator invites the group to consider where the differences in the scores occurred and why people scored differently for each area.
   b. Group members explain and justify ratings. For example, a group may say, "We thought that rating was a one because. . ." and cite evidence from the document review or data analysis.
   c. Discuss any area where there is a discrepancy in the rating, resolving issues until consensus is reached. Given that the overall ratings are district-based, discrepancies sometimes result because a driver is in place at one school and may not be in place at another. If this occurs, change the overall rating to partially or mostly in place because it may be present at some sites in the district but not all sites.
3. Debrief: Summarize the areas that are fully in place, mostly in place, partially, and not in place yet to ensure agreement. This step will help build a collective understanding of what will be necessary to focus on in developing an MTSS action plan.

Instructional Vision

This section is small and easy to overlook, but it is the heart of the work. Here you are articulating your collective understanding of what instruction should look like in practice (see Table 7.1). Throughout the self-assessment, we reference a set of effective instructional practices. In our work, this is defined as the use of pedagogy rooted in deeper learning and

Table 7.1 MTSS vision self-assessment.

Instructional Vision	
Summary	In this section you will examine your instructional vision and the degree to which it is grounded in deeper learning and equity, and shared across the learning community.
Focus Area	Refining what high-quality instruction looks like.
Guiding Question	What is our instructional vision?
Equity Pause	• Does your vision lend itself to equitable and rigorous student outcomes for all learners? • How did your educators', students', and families' perspectives inform your vision? • How are strategies for equity—at the individual, institutional, or systems level—built into the vision?
Indicators	Instructional Vision • **Shared vision:** The learning community has a shared understanding of high-quality instruction, which promotes deeper learning for all students. • **Grounded in equity:** The instructional vision is grounded in equity, communicates high expectations, and advances equitable outcomes for all learners. • **Student experience:** The vision centers around the student experience and creates conditions for student engagement and agency in their own learning.

UDL, evidence-based practice, culturally sustaining practice, the use of high-quality instructional materials, linguistically supportive practice, the inclusion of standards-based instruction, and trauma-informed practice. The combination of these practices in all settings serves as a foundation for which all students can be successful in our schools.

Pause and Reflect

After reviewing the core components of an instructional vision that drives inclusive and equitable MTSS, reflect on your current vision. Do you have a shared vision, grounded in equity and the student experience? What rating would you provide for your vision as it relates to what you have learned about MTSS, deeper learning and UDL?

- (0) Not yet in place
- (1) Partially in place
- (2) Mostly in place
- (3) Fully in place

Instructional Design

In this section, we will look at our learning environment and the implementation of the instructional vision. You can use this self-assessment to answer this question: "How far are we from our vision?" Think of this process as the beginning bridge between where you are and where you want to be. Table 7.2 summarizes sample components of this part of a self-assessment. For each indicator, consider your alignment on a rating scale like the one previously shared.

Table 7.2 MTSS instructional design self-assessment.

Instructional Design	
Summary	This section includes elements of the learning environment and implementing the vision in practice. This section will help you identify ways you might strengthen high-impact components of instructional design and move closer to instructional practices that embody deeper learning.
Focus Area	The student learning experience is rooted in deeper learning, universally designed, supported by evidence-based instruction using high-quality instructional materials, and is consistently implemented for all students.
Guiding Question	How well does our vision show up in our daily practice and classroom experience?
Equity Pause	• Do the implemented materials and assessments create unnecessary barriers for students? • What does student work show about the progress toward the instructional vision? • Are there differences in how specific students or student populations experience our instructional design?
Indicators	Curricular Materials • **High-quality instructional materials:** Materials are bias-free, have empirical evidence of efficacy (high-quality instructional materials, HQIM), engaging content, and are inclusive in design. • **Coherence:** Materials used across all three tiers exhibit a coherent sequence of target skills and knowledge that advances deeper learning (i.e., vertically and horizontally aligned). • **Vision alignment:** The learning community has a system for reviewing curricular materials and adjusting as needed to align to the instructional vision.

(Continued)

Table 7.2   **(Continued)**

Instructional Design

Equitable Practices
- **Equitable access:** All students receive challenging, grade-appropriate instruction and have equitable access to effective instructional practices.
- **MLL support:** All multilingual learners have access to appropriate language development services as part of a Tier 1 instruction that is culturally responsive. Additionally, all multilingual learners are provided with opportunities to develop and practice discipline-specific language.
- **SWD/504 support:** Instructional practices outlined in the 504 or IEP used with students with disabilities must be research-based, provide equitable access to Tier 1 instruction, and be implemented with fidelity.

Pedagogy
- **Effective instructional practices:** The learning community implements effective instructional practices (rooted in deeper learning, universally designed, culturally sustaining, linguistically supportive, and trauma-informed).
- **Implementation:** The organization has identified measures and resources (e.g., observation tools or an instructional guide) to ensure organization-wide fidelity.
- **High expectations:** There are high expectations for all students across all classrooms, including multilingual learners and students with disabilities such that students are engaging with grade-level work that advances deeper learning.

Table 7.2   (Continued)

Instructional Design

Assessment
- **Data-informed practice:** Standards-based and universally designed formative and summative assessments are used to monitor student progress toward learning goals and to inform effective instructional support.
- **Data-based decisions:** There is a process for collecting and analyzing student work throughout units to monitor student performance that results in increasing equitable outcomes.
- **Engagement:** Each student's strengths, progress, and next steps are shared with students and families such that students and families know and can track their progress.

Learning Environment
- **Safety:** The learning environment is physically and psychologically safe, supportive, and accessible.
- **Belonging:** Students experience a learning environment that recognizes the value of all educators and students and is inclusive in nature.
- **Feedback:** The organization utilizes ongoing feedback cycles from students, families/caregivers, community partners, and educators to build an inclusive, positive school community.

Pause and Reflect

As you consider the instructional design in your school or district, what strengths and areas of need have you identified? Consider each of the components and reflect on how you would rate your curricular materials, equitable practices, pedagogy, assessments, and learning environments as they relate to the development of an inclusive and equitable MTSS.

- (0) Not yet in place
- (1) Partially in place
- (2) Mostly in place
- (3) Fully in place

Tiered Systems

In this next section, we focus on the implementation of multi-tiered systems of support through tiered systems and the creation of a robust data culture (see Table 7.3).

Table 7.3 Tiered systems self-assessment.

Tiered Systems	
Summary	This part of the self-assessment explores components of tiered systems for students and effective data systems that are important for ensuring that all students can access deeper learning.
Focus Area	The organization uses an MTSS model to provide a tiered and fluid continuum of evidence-based academic and social emotional/behavioral supports and interventions for all students at universal (Tier 1), targeted (Tier 2), and intensive (Tier 3) levels.
Guiding Question	How well do we ensure that all students have equitable access to our instructional vision?
Equity Pause	• What progress is being made toward your vision, disaggregated by specific student groups? • Are certain student populations overrepresented in particular tiers of support and/or in the referral process? What potential biases and/or blind spots might be contributing to overrepresentation? • How do adults examine their own biases and blind spots and their effects in relation to the vision? What biases and blind spots are coming up as part of the work?

Table 7.3 (Continued)

Tiered Systems

Indicators	Tiered Supports

- **Domains:** There is a systemic approach to developing a comprehensive set of tiered supports for all learners across all three domains (academic, social/emotional, and behavioral).
- **Tiered interventions:** The organization creates conditions and systems to provide universal (Tier 1), targeted (Tier 2), and intensive (Tier 3) support to students.
- **MLL:** All multilingual learners receive appropriate language development services, access to Tier 1 instruction, and can access a tiered system of support, as needed.
- **Students with Disabilities (SWDs):** IEPs are designed and implemented to ensure that all SWDs can access scientifically based tiered support as appropriate in the least restrictive environment.
- **Engagement in student support:** Families/caregivers and students are actively engaged in student support processes/decisions and are regularly informed about progress. Families/caregivers receive the information they need to advocate for their children and are informed of their rights to request a special education evaluation at any time during the tiered support process.

Data-Driven

- **Data systems:** All schools have a clear system and process of collecting and distributing universal screening, diagnostic, and progress monitoring to inform placement and progress within their tiered system of support.
- **Assessment plans:** All schools have an assessment plan that defines the purpose, type, and timing of all school-wide and districtwide assessments, including universal screeners, diagnostic assessments, and progress monitoring tools (across all three domains). The map is reviewed regularly to ensure that it is accessible to all as well as culturally and linguistically appropriate.

(Continued)

Table 7.3   (Continued)

Tiered Systems

- **Data-driven culture:** Leaders and educators create/ embrace a culture that centers on using triangulated data to assess and address current systems that create barriers for students.
- **Student needs:** Administrators, teachers, students, and families/caregivers engage in strategic problem-solving processes that identify student needs and determine progress monitoring protocols for short- and long-term goals. This includes students with diverse needs such as those with IEPs and 504 plans, as well as multilingual learners.

Access to Resources

- **Reviews:** A regular review of student needs is conducted at least annually to ensure that student needs drive staffing and service structures, as opposed to retrofitting student needs into existing models or assessing positions and/or roles that no longer meet the needs of current students or models that may be contributing to inequity.
- **Tiered staffing:** The staffing selection, models, and positions are designed to support the implementation of MTSS based on students' needs. Consideration is given to staff titles and duties to foster a positive approach to meeting the needs of all students. Staff is (re)allocated based on student needs annually and during the year.
- **Tiered scheduling:** The schedule articulates when tiered supports will occur, ensures that intervention services are supplemental and not supplanting core instruction, specifies priorities to direct student supports in staff schedules, and provides time to administer and review data to identify and monitor students.

Table 7.3   (Continued)

Tiered Systems

- **Community partnerships:** Community partners are actively engaged to better support students and families/caregivers and to connect them to social services related to health, social, recreational, and supplemental educational services.
- **Technology:** Educational and assistive technology is available for all students and used in alignment with the instructional vision and to increase access to appropriate tiered supports.

Pause and Reflect

As you consider the tiered supports in your school or district, what strengths and areas of need have you identified? Consider each of the indicators and reflect on how you would rate your tiered systems of support, data-driven practices, and student access to resources as they relate to the development of an inclusive and equitable MTSS.

- (0) Not yet in place
- (1) Partially in place
- (2) Mostly in place
- (3) Fully in place

Systems and Structures

We have to support our instructional practices and tiered supports with systems and structures. This section ensures that we create and sustain an integrated system that results in our vision for all learners. It focuses on the processes and resources in place to communicate, support, and improve practices to realize the instructional vision. Here, you continue your self-assessment by understanding where you are as an organization. You will do this by conducting this portion of the self-assessment by referencing content in Table 7.4.

Table 7.4　Systems and structures self-assessment.

Systems and Structures	
Summary	This final set of components explore the foundational aspects such as staff development and competency, improvement cycles, and resource allocation, which we can leverage to sustain a longer-term vision of deeper learning.
Focus Area	The organization utilizes its systems and structures to prioritize and allocate its people, time, technology, funding, and so on in service of the instructional vision. This results in optimizing tiered systems needed to support all students.
Guiding Question	How well do our systems and structures support our instructional vision?
Equity Pause	• How does the culture support personal and professional learning in relation to the instructional vision? • How do adults learn in your schools? How does this mirror your vision (or not)? • To what extent does the learning community reflect on and confront inherent biases and blind spots in their collaboration and processes? What is the outcome of that reflection? • How do we honor all voices at the decision-making and implementation stages of our programming? For example, what do we do to ensure representative stakeholders and invite multiple voices and perspectives into our processes? • To what extent do teams have the autonomy and information to make decisions?

Table 7.4 (Continued)

Systems and Structures

Indicators   Staff Development and Competency

- **Professional learning plan:** The organization has a sustainable professional learning plan that offers coherent high-quality, universally designed professional development that is informed by and results in movement toward the instructional vision.

- **High-quality professional learning:** Educators engage in data-based and relevant ongoing, job-embedded professional learning opportunities, including frequent observations and feedback that advance skillful use of high-quality curricular materials and associated educational technology. Professional learning results in effective instructional practices that advance deeper learning and include tiered coaching models.

- **Collaborative planning:** There is time in the schedule for educators (including interventionists, ESL instructors, and special educators) with designated opportunities to collaborate, analyze data and student work, assess the effectiveness of instruction, plan, and engage in learning experiences that deepen their understanding and implementation of effective instructional practices and provide access to grade-appropriate content for all students.

- **Observation and feedback:** All schools and/or teams have routines and systems for frequent observation and feedback that focus on clearly defined and communicated expectations for effective instructional practices to advance deeper learning.

- **Evaluation:** There are strategic, unbiased, and transparent systems for evaluation, using student feedback, observation data, and review of artifacts along to make informed decisions about opportunities for educator support and leadership development.

(Continued)

Table 7.4   (Continued)

Systems and Structures

Structural Support
- **Alignment to vision:** Resources are strategically aligned for impact and informed by data, and allocations are vetted with a lens toward access and equity; the alignment between resources and the instructional vision is well articulated.
- **Fiscal support:** The budget provides appropriate levels of funding for high-quality instructional and intervention materials and assessments, key positions, professional development, and so on.
- **Structural review:** Policies, practices, and procedures are analyzed with an equity lens, such as a review for disproportionality for students of color or accessing the language accessibility of the assessment for multilingual learners.
- **Technology:** There is a clear and consistent process for selecting and evaluating technology products that are aligned to the instructional vision and responsive to student and staff needs.

Continuous Improvement Cycles
- **Leadership commitment:** There is an active leadership team that takes on the responsibility of ensuring that systems meet the needs of all learners. The team has the authority to make resource, scheduling, programmatic, and staffing decisions and has representation from a range of leaders (e.g., academics, student support, special education, and multilingual learners).
- **Continuous improvement:** The organization engages in ongoing and inclusive long-term (multiyear and annual) and short-term (quarterly and monthly) goal setting and monitoring toward realizing the instructional vision and ensuring each student is making progress, which results in adjustments to the school's structures, programs, and resources (e.g., time, staff, schedules) throughout the year.

Table 7.4   (Continued)

Systems and Structures

- **Representation:** Voices from all students, families, and communities are used to drive improvement efforts and obtain perceptual data on the progress of the plan. Representation is assessed to ensure participation and engagement represent the community at large, with a specific lens to remove barriers to participation (e.g., transportation or language barriers).
- **Equity focused:** Improvement efforts are grounded in concepts of equity and identify clear goals to close the opportunity gap for all students (including MLLs, SWDs, newcomers, SLIFE, ELSWDs, etc.).
- **Multiyear planning:** A multiyear district strategy process is established and results in a multiyear plan rooted in implementation science. The district plan informs annual district action plans, school improvement plans, and educator goals. Annual action plans include the use of benchmarks to access progress toward the improvement goals.
- **Midcourse corrections and continuous improvement:** Based on the data collected through fidelity measures and feedback loops, decisions are made about how to enhance the effectiveness of the work.

Human Resources
- **Distributive leadership:** The organization has instructional leadership teams or equivalent structures to collaboratively develop and reflect on the effectiveness of professional development, planning, and implementation efforts. Across the organization, team and collaboration structures create shared responsibility and ownership and have an impact on school improvement.

(Continued)

Table 7.4   (Continued)

Systems and Structures

- **Hiring:** Hiring processes and procedures are bias-free and ensure that all candidates have the relevant expertise to meet each student's needs and have a mindset and belief that all students can learn at high levels. The organization systematically reviews staff hiring processes and policies to ensure that they are nondiscriminatory, inclusive, and focused on meeting the needs of all learners.
- **Retention:** Hiring and retention policies and procedures include strategies to recruit, mentor, train, and support a diverse educator and administrator workforce that is well-prepared to teach culturally and linguistically diverse students.

Pause and Reflect

As you consider the systems and structures in your school or district, what strengths and areas of need have you identified? Consider each of the indicators and reflect on how you would rate your staff development and competency, structural support, continuous improvement cycles, and human resources as they relate to the development of an inclusive and equitable MTSS.

- (0) Not yet in place
- (1) Partially in place
- (2) Mostly in place
- (3) Fully in place

Key Findings

Based on your initiatives review, document review, asset-mapping, data review, and self-assessment, what are the top three to five key findings? Let's start with associated readiness elements and essential planning questions. Table 7.5 shows those aligned with all components of our equitable MTSS model. You can use these essential planning questions to help you focus on your key findings.

Table 7.5 Readiness elementary and essential planning questions.

Readiness Elements	Essential Planning Questions
Vision	
Instructional Vision	Does the organization have a clear vision for instruction rooted in deeper learning, inclusive in nature, supported by evidence-based instructional practice and materials, and articulated and understood by everyone at the implementation level?
Instructional Design	
Instructional Foundations	Does the organization use high-quality instructional materials, have coherence across materials, and use assessments to monitor student performance to inform instructional practice?
Instructional Implementation	Is there evidence of the use of effective instructional practices (pedagogy rooted in deeper learning and UDL, evidence-based practice, culturally sustaining practice, the use of high-quality instructional materials, linguistically supportive practice, the inclusion of standards-based instruction, and trauma-informed practice) at all levels?
Equitable Practice	Do all students receive challenging, grade-appropriate instruction and have equitable access to effective instructional practices, including multilingual learners and students with disabilities?
Learning Environment	Is the learning environment safe physically and psychologically (e.g., gives a sense of belonging, provides a sense of agency, and recognizes the value of all educators and students)?

(Continued)

Table 7.5   (Continued)

Readiness Elements	Essential Planning Questions
Tiered Systems	
Tiered Support	Does the district/school use an MTSS model to provide a tiered continuum of evidence-based academic support for all students at universal (Tier 1), targeted (Tier 2), and intensive (Tier 3) levels?
Data Systems	Does the district/school have clear systems and procedures to support educator teams in using formative and summative assessment data for screening, diagnostic, and progress monitoring purposes?
Foundational Resources	Does the organization have the appropriate foundational resources necessary to support a tiered system of support such as tiered scheduling, staffing, and a regular cycle of programmatic reviews?
Systems and Structures	
Staff Attainment, Development and Competency	Does our organization hire the best staff to meet the needs of our students, and when hired do we provide appropriate supports for staff success such as high-quality professional learning, collaborative planning structures, and mastery-oriented feedback?
Structural Supports	As an organization focused on equitable MTSS, do our fiscal allocation, chosen technology, policies, procedures, and practices align with our instructional vision?
Continuous Improvement Cycles	Do we engage in improvement planning that is based on implementation science and improvement science, and includes a lens on equity and planning team representation?

Sometimes we feel overwhelmed by this process. One way to think about this is by using the self-assessment readiness elements articulated previously. For example, if we find a lot of low scores in a particular section, what is the readiness element for that section of the self-assessment? Let's go through an example.

In a recent self-assessment, we found a lot of indicators were 0 or 1 under instructional implementation. So we reviewed the essential planning question under that readiness element. It read, "Does the organization have a clear vision for instruction that is rooted in deeper learning, inclusive in nature, supported by evidence-based instructional practice and materials, and articulated and understood by everyone at the implementation level?" We knew the organization did not, based on the self-assessment results, so we turned that into a finding by stating, "There is not a clear vision for instruction that is rooted in deeper learning, inclusive in nature, supported by evidence-based instructional practice and materials, and articulated and understood by everyone at the implementation level."

Key findings will focus your work in the upcoming planning cycle and will support you in prioritizing upcoming action steps. This step intends to organize your data and self-assessment to prioritize areas for improvement planning. Table 7.6 shows sample key findings with subfindings informed by each section of the self-assessment.

Summary

The self-assessment process is designed to help district teams assess the systems and structures they have in place already and those they do not have yet, to foster an effective and equitable MTSS that supports all students. Using the document and data review to complete the self-assessment is critical to identifying key findings that will drive the improvement process. As with all other steps in this process, transparency and communication are key. Once key findings are identified, they should be shared with multiple stakeholders and other district teams for feedback.

Reflection Questions

1. How has reviewing the self-assessment resources in this chapter changed your understanding of MTSS?

2. Consider your current process for completing a needs assessment as it relates to MTSS. What are the strengths of your current process? What will you improve in future strategic cycles?

3. How would this self-assessment process help to build a shared understanding of the strengths and areas in need of improvement in your school or district as it relates to MTSS?

4. Once you complete the self-assessment process, how will you share a draft of the results with all stakeholders for review and feedback?

Table 7.6   Sample key findings.

Key Finding

There is not a shared instructional vision understood by all staff, such as through an articulated instructional guide, that details a common set of evidence-based, standards-aligned, universally designed, culturally sustaining, linguistically supportive, and trauma-informed instructional strategies, rooted in deeper learning.

Instructional Design Subfindings

- Not all of our materials can be categorized as high-quality instructional materials: materials that are bias-free, have empirical evidence of efficacy (high-quality instructional materials/HQIM), include engaging content, and are inclusive in design.
- There is no instructional guide to articulate expectations about the use of high-quality instructional practices.
- The learning community has not yet consistently implemented effective instructional practices (rooted in deeper learning, universally designed, culturally sustaining, linguistically supportive, and trauma-informed).
- The organization has not identified measures and resources (e.g., observation tools or an instructional guide) to ensure organization-wide fidelity of high-quality instructional practices.
- There is no process for collecting and analyzing student work throughout units to monitor student performance that increases equitable outcomes.

8

Root-Cause Analysis

In this chapter, we discuss the importance of root-cause analysis to better understand why the system produces the current outcomes. When you can target root causes, you can address them through strategic planning. Root cause analysis is a multistep process that requires identifying potential root causes, organizing root causes around control, and validating and verifying those causes. This chapter will prepare you to complete a root-cause analysis after you organize the key findings from your self-assessment process.

Down the River

Once upon a time, a group of adults enjoyed the sun on the bank of a river. Suddenly, they heard screaming. They whipped around and saw a teenager getting pulled down that river, splashing around frantically, yelling for help. Immediately, they sprang into action, racing to the water and bringing the teen to safety. They felt proud of their collective effort and maybe a little judgmental. They whispered to themselves, "Why would he go into the water if he wasn't a strong swimmer? Someone should talk to his mother."

Strangely, the same thing happened minutes later. Another teenager was struggling to make it ashore, thrashing in the water. "Kids these days," they thought, "We need to find out who their parents are and get them some life preservers. What a terrible decision to swim in the river without a life jacket." A third child floated down the river, the adults becoming increasingly tired as they rescued the teens. One of the women finally walked off. The others were disgusted. "How could she leave us here to deal with all these irresponsible teenagers?" The remaining friends continued to stay vigilant, perched above the river, ready to dive in. Before they knew it, the woman returned.

"Where did you go?" they asked.

She answered, "I walked down the river, and about a mile back, the bridge is broken. That is where the kids fall in. Come with me so we can fix that."

Identify Potential Root Causes

The previous story reminds us that sometimes we have to look a little deeper to figure out why something has occurred. Through this process thus far, you have drafted key findings and are ready to dive in to rescue the swimmers! Not quite. It is time for you to walk down the metaphorical river and complete a root-cause analysis. Root-cause analysis is a process where you further define and understand the problem that will focus improvement efforts. Root-cause analysis moves the team from a broad problem to one that is specific enough on which to act (Rowland et al., 2018).

The self-assessment process helps identify key findings. For example, one of your key findings may be that there is not adequate professional development to support staff in designing universally designed, culturally sustaining, linguistically supportive, and trauma-informed lessons rooted in deeper learning. It is easy to look at the lack of professional development and say, "That's the problem! All we need is a few more hours of PD, and all will be well with the world." Instead, we need to dive deeply into why we do not have professional development that prepares educators to meet the needs of all learners.

A root-cause analysis is intended to find the antecedents for your key findings. It digs into structural domains by focusing on cause and effect. In this stage, look at factors associated with each finding. We have provided a set of those factors in our self-assessment to help take the guesswork out of this process. Let's examine how a key finding may unfold through a root-cause analysis in Table 8.1.

Table 8.1 Sample of root-cause analysis.

Categories of Effects (Drawn from the Ratings on the Self-Assessment)	Potential Root Causes (Drawn from the Data and Document Review)
Curriculum • Why are there holes in our use of high-quality instructional materials (HQIM)?	There are no district-vetted and defined process, protocols, or rubrics used during curriculum adoption that define the qualities of HQIM.
Pedagogy • Why hasn't the full learning community implemented effective instructional practices (rooted in deeper learning, universally designed, culturally sustaining, linguistically supportive, and trauma-informed) consistently?	There is no definition of instructional practice and no guide to articulate these expectations. In addition, the organization has not identified measures and resources (e.g., observation tools or an instructional guide) to ensure organization-wide fidelity of high-quality instructional practices.
Assessment • There is no process for collecting and analyzing student work throughout units to monitor student performance to increase equitable outcomes.	There is no common planning time embedded into the schedule. There are no established protocols for analyzing student work. There has been no PD on how to use student work to inform instructional design.

As shown in Table 8.1, you can use the self-assessment process to help identify the effects of your systems and root-cause analysis (with information gathered from your data and document review) to articulate potential root causes. Sometimes we review documents and data, and they inform our thinking, and sometimes the absence of documents and data provides just as healthy a source of planning information. In this case, the lack of an instructional guide was a potential antecedent for the key finding.

Pause and Reflect

Take a moment to reflect on the integration of previous steps in this process and your root-cause analysis. Note how this process brings together results from the needs assessment which included the document review and data analysis as well as the self-assessment to determine potential root causes. Why is it important that the team commit to each step in this process instead of jumping into setting strategic goals?

Organizing Your Proposed Root Causes Around Control

Once you have identified potential root causes, categorize them into three "piles" (see Figure 8.1):

- Pile 1: Those causes within your locus of control. These are things we can change without outside permission.
- Pile 2: Those not in your direct locus of control but within your sphere of influence. These are things we do not have a direct say in but have influence around.
- Pile 3: Outside your locus of control/sphere of influence. These are things that we cannot control but may impact our organization.

This step is important as you consider your action plan. First, you must consider actions that the team can address with autonomy. Next, you want

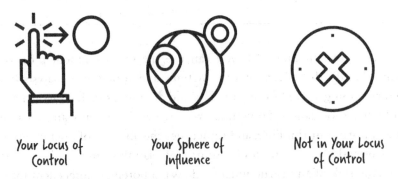

Your Locus of   Your Sphere of   Not in Your Locus
Control   Influence   of Control

Figure 8.1   Three piles of control.

to consider actions in your plans for collaboration and engagement with all relevant stakeholders for items within your sphere of influence. Lastly, you need to understand the impact of causes that fall outside your control and plan accordingly.

Let's play out two scenarios to illustrate the distinctions in those piles.

> **Scenario 1.** You identify lack of funding for intervention materials as a root cause. Is this in your locus of control, your sphere of influence, or outside your control? Specifically, do you have funds within your existing general fund budget that can be applied to intervention resources (within your sphere of control), do you need to advocate through the town(s) budget process for additional budget appropriations to support intervention acquisition (within your sphere of influence), or are you in a position of waiting to see annual entitlement fund distributions from the state to see if you have funds to purchase the materials (outside your control)?
>
> **Scenario 2.** As a school-based team, do you have the power to determine the intervention materials once funding is approved (locus of control), or do you need to work with another group who needs to approve the materials (sphere of influence), or are intervention resources provided to you with no input from your team (outside your control)?

Review Root Causes for Leverage

It is important to consider how to assess our potential root causes against the concept of leverage.

- **High leverage:** an area where a small/moderate amount of "lift" (work) will greatly impact outcomes.
- **Low leverage:** an area where there is a ton of "lift" for a very small gain.

For example, if we define something as a potential root cause but the impact is only in one grade in one school, this is less likely to impact systemic planning and may be better suited as a goal for that grade-level team. In addition, you want to look at the lift (or level of effort and resources) needed to address this root cause. With limited resources, if a cause has low impact and high lift, should it be prioritized in your planning? Figure 8.2 will help you visualize the tension between leverage and lift.

Through discussion, determine which root causes are high leverage and within your locus of control/sphere of influence. These will be the causes you bring forward to the validation and verification process.

Validate Your Root Causes

During the validation step, take the potential root causes and share them with greater stakeholder members. To do this, you need to plan. In other words, how will you solicit feedback about your potential root causes and from whom to ensure there is agreement and buy-in about district needs? For example, maybe you will create a survey or host focus groups with students, staff, and families.

When we worked in a district together, we visited every school during an established faculty meeting to share key findings and root causes with faculty and staff. We wrote the key findings from our data analysis at the top of a piece of paper. We listed all of our potential root causes (those within our locus of control and medium or high leverage areas) in separate

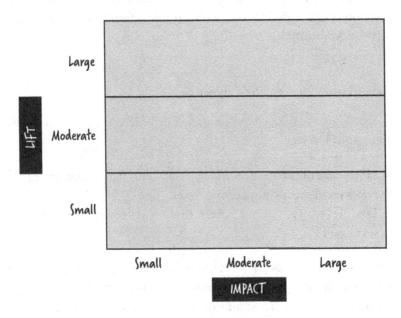

Figure 8.2 Leverage versus lift.

spreadsheet rows. We asked participants to review the key findings and, from their perspective, determine if they agreed that the potential root cause was a factor in our challenge area. We asked them to write notes with examples if they agreed or a rationale for why they did not agree. We gave them the option to work individually or in small groups to complete the validation process. This was a powerful way to validate root causes and create shared responsibility for strategic changes. See a recording sheet sample in Table 8.2.

Table 8.2   Root cause validation recording sheet sample.

Key Findings
There is not a shared instructional vision understood by all staff, such as through an articulated instructional guide, that details a common set of evidence-based, standards-aligned, universally designed, culturally sustaining, linguistically supportive, and trauma-informed instructional strategies, rooted in deeper learning.

Potential Root Cause	Do You Agree? "Y" for yes or "N" for no	Notes
There are no district-vetted and defined process, protocols, or rubrics used during curriculum adoption that speak to the qualities of HQIM.		
There is no definition of instructional practice and no guide to articulate these expectations. In addition, the organization has not identified measures and resources (e.g., observation tools or an instructional guide) to ensure organization-wide fidelity of high-quality instructional practices.		
There is no common planning time embedded into the schedule. There are no established protocols for analyzing student work. There has been no PD on how to effectively use student work to inform instructional design.		

Verify Your Root Causes

For each validated root cause, your task is to go back with your team and find data to support it. It is best to triangulate the data (find three separate sources) to ensure the root cause is an accurate antecedent to your challenge area. If there is no data to support your root cause, you need to let it go from your work moving forward. This can be challenging, but sometimes what we believe is not necessarily the actual antecedent, as shown in the following scenario.

> **Scenario:** Your team determines that lack of PD time in inclusive practice and deeper learning impacts student achievement. Your staff validates this root cause and desires additional time for PD. To verify it, you review time spent on PD against research-based hours, collect qualitative data from staff through surveys and additional focus groups, and compare your PD time to districts with strong outcomes with similar student profiles. What you find is that the time itself may not be the problem. There is adequate time for professional learning, but teachers do not find value in the PD, or they aren't supported to implement the practices introduced in PD due to the lack of a robust educator evaluation system and instructional coaching. If you did not engage in this process, you might be focusing on the wrong action item for your plan, and increased time would not necessarily impact your outcomes as you had wished.

For each validated root cause, determine data sets that you will review to determine their accuracy. You can complete the grid, like the one in Table 8.3, if you think it is a helpful tool.

Table 8.3 Sample verification template.

Key Finding			
Validated Root Causes	Data Source #1	Data Source #2	Data Source #3

Summary

The process of district-wide change is complex. We have to create a committed team, develop a shared vision, and complete a thorough needs assessment process that includes reviewing current initiatives, document review, data analysis and mapping, and a self-assessment. Once this process is complete, we establish key findings but must dig deeper to determine, verify, and validate root causes. Although this may seem cumbersome, it is absolutely essential. Reflect on the story we introduced at the beginning of the chapter. All the rescue equipment in the world would not address the problem of the broken bridge. We have to explore multiple data sources and ask, "Why are we experiencing these outcomes?" more times than we think we should if we are going to target the areas that will impact all our learners.

Reflection Questions

1. Have you completed a root-cause analysis in your previous strategic cycles? Compare your past practices with the methodology outlined in this chapter.
2. How will you share your key findings and potential root causes with all stakeholders to increase transparency and buy-in?
3. Why is verifying root causes critical before drafting strategic goals and an action plan for MTSS and district improvement?
4. What strategies could you use to validate your root causes?

9

Planning for Success

In this chapter, we will support you in transforming your needs assessment process into a strategic plan that aims to build an inclusive and equitable MTSS that supports all students. The foundational work that was outlined in previous chapters will ensure that your strategic goals and action steps address areas of need and the root causes of your current outcomes. You will learn about the importance of creating logic models to drive district improvement throughout your strategic planning process.

Walk with Me (Kristan)

I am not sure where I was, but it was somewhere remote, and I was young. I looked down, and my knuckles were protruding from my fist as it wrapped around a large rope. My trembling fingers were attached to a cable that supported a set of boards that formed a large bridge high in the air. In my little mind, there was no way I was crossing the bridge. It moved with the wind and was unsteady below my feet. Just as I was resolved to walk away, I heard my father's voice call to me.

"It's okay," he said. "I am here. Just walk to me." My faith in him must have been stronger than my fear because I began to move across the bridge. After making it safely onto the other side, my legs felt like jelly. But I had done it, I had crossed. There have been so many times in my professional career when I felt like that little girl again. I stood unsure if I should move ahead.

Always, though, I had the aid of guides. My sherpas may have been my conscience, my students, or my colleagues, but each time, they helped me over the chasm. In this chapter, we create a bridge—a bridge between our vision of deeper learning and an improvement planning process grounded in science. Let's take that first step together! As my dad said, "It's okay. I am here. Just walk to me."

Strategic Planning Process

In a systems-level planning framework such as MTSS, it is essential for there to be a call to action. This is best done with a multiyear and well-thought-out district strategy. A multiyear district strategy process is established and results in a multiyear plan rooted in implementation science. The district plan informs annual district action plans, school improvement plans, and educator goals.

The district strategy process must be implemented with a lens toward coherence and representation. Table 9.1 is a set of conditions that the team can use to engage in the planning process. These components were drawn from the appendix of our *Coherence Guidebook* (Massachusetts Department of Elementary and Secondary Education, 2022).

Pause and Reflect

As you consider your MTSS team and your work to create a strategic plan, do you have the conditions in Table 9.1 present? If so, how do you know? If any of the conditions are missing, how will you go about collaborating with stakeholders to recognize areas of need and continue to build the necessary conditions for success?

Strategic Plan

A strategic plan is the guiding document that creates the explicit improvement planning work that the district will focus on. It will become the cornerstone of all budgeting, planning, and staffing conversations across the organization. The strategic plan operationalizes the district's vision. The

Table 9.1   Conditions to review strategic planning process.

Components	Sample Action Steps
Leadership commitment: There is an active leadership team that takes responsibility for ensuring that systems meet the needs of all learners. The team has the authority to make resource, scheduling, programmatic, and staffing decisions and has representation from a range of leaders (e.g., academics, student support, special education).	Create a schedule for the improvement planning process to be integrated into existing district and school leadership team meetings on a consistent basis.
Continuous improvement: The organization engages in ongoing and inclusive long-term (multiyear and annual) and short-term (quarterly and monthly) goal setting and monitoring toward realizing the instructional vision and ensuring each student is making progress, which results in adjustments to the school's structures, programs, and resources (e.g., time, staff, schedules) throughout the year.	Draft a multi-year improvement plan. Create the annual feedback measures based on the plan's priority areas.
Representation: Voices from all students, families, and communities are used to drive improvement efforts and obtain perception data on the plan's progress. Representation is assessed to ensure participation and engagement represent the community at large, with a specific lens to remove barriers to participation (e.g., transportation or language barriers).	Include specific questions focused on the improvement plan's priority areas in an annual family/caregiver survey.
Equity focused: Improvement efforts are grounded in concepts of equity and identify clear goals to close the opportunity gap for all students (including MLLs, SWDs, newcomers, SLIFE, ELSWDs, etc.).	Conduct an annual equity review and use the findings to inform improvement plan action steps.

(Continued)

Table 9.1   (Continued)

Components	Sample Action Steps
Multiyear planning: A multiyear district strategy process is established and results in a multiyear plan rooted in implementation science. The district plan informs annual district action plans, school improvement plans, and educator goals. Annual action plans include the use of benchmarks to assess progress toward the improvement goals.	Publish an annual assessment map that is inclusive of quantitative and qualitative measures. Define the three-year plan's target benchmarks with data drawn from student outcomes data, instructional data, perspectives data, and systems/structures data.
Midcourse corrections and continuous improvement: Based on the data collected through fidelity measures and feedback loops, decisions are made about how to enhance the effectiveness of the work.	Create and share a set of defined data protocols and data points that will be used by the improvement planning team to guide their work.

language in Table 9.2 is intended to give you a sample of what your district strategy language *may* look like. This strategic language is not meant to be inclusive. Rather, it shows how different components we discussed throughout this text build on each other in a coherent way.

   Each district will have its own unique strengths, challenges, and plans and thus the organization of the district strategic and the corresponding language will be unique to each district.

Table 9.2   Sample strategy language.

Sample Theory of Action	If we implement a multi-tiered system of support built on a foundation of Universal Design for Learning and equity and access that is inclusive of academic support, behavioral systems, and social emotional learning, then we will reach our vision of guiding students to learn today, lead tomorrow, and reach the world.
Sample Objective Statement	In order to increase achievement for all students, we will develop and implement a multi-tiered system of support with a focus on high-quality curriculum, Universal Design for Learning (UDL), culturally and linguistically supportive practices, and evidence-based instruction and intervention.
Sample Initiatives	• We will develop and deliver a comprehensive and equitable tiered instructional model focused on academic excellence. • We will develop and deliver a comprehensive tiered support model focused on the social emotional and mental health of all students. • We will develop and deliver a comprehensive tiered behavioral support framework.
Sample Goals	• 5-Year Plan Example: By June 20★★, all students will receive equitable access to universally designed high-quality instruction in inclusive classrooms, as measured by a district scope and sequence, curriculum material reviews, classroom walkthroughs using a peer-reviewed tool, student schedules, and increased student outcomes. • 3-Year Example: By June 20★★, to increase the achievement level and growth of 100% of accountability groups, all teachers will analyze results from a variety of assessments to determine progress toward intended outcomes and use these findings to adjust practice and identify and/or implement differentiated interventions and enhancements for students, as measured by meeting notes, observation data, and increased overall performance levels standardized tests and district benchmark assessments.

(Continued)

Table 9.2   (Continued)

Sample Measurable Annual Goals	• Meet all state accountability targets for all students and high-risk subgroups. • 80% of observed classrooms will be implementing universally designed instructional strategies related to critical thinking, creativity, communication, and collaboration. • Achieve a 15% increase in the equity review results in relation to the percentage of SWD who are placed in higher-level courses as compared to last year. • Administer districtwide benchmark and common assessments aligned to scope and sequence to all students twice a year.
Sample Interim Benchmarks for Educators/ Practitioners	• 100% of scope and sequence documents are standards-aligned for ELA and math departments. • 80% of curricular review documents (units and lesson plans) will include the UDL principles and relevant standards. • Each month, starting from the beginning of the year, all collaborative teams will analyze data for strengths and challenges, identify actions to address student learning needs, and regularly communicate and follow up on action steps, as evidenced by meeting notes, observations, and staff feedback. • Pilot schedules in the **** school year that includes a daily intervention block for all students to supplement and not supplant inclusive Tier 1 classrooms. • 80% of observed classrooms will be implementing universally designed instructional strategies during the intervention block.

Table 9.2 (Continued)

	• Each month, starting from the beginning of the year, all collaborative teams will analyze data for strengths and challenges, identify actions to address student learning needs, and regularly communicate and follow up on action steps, as evidenced by meeting notes, observations, and staff feedback. • We will establish, codify, and share data to inform a continuous cycle of improvement where all teachers participate in monthly data meetings and incorporate findings from those data meetings into the design of more inclusive universally designed lessons. • We will ensure that we meet the needs of all students and write intervention plans for all students scoring below the 40th percentile for use during the intervention block.
Sample Interim Benchmarks for Students	• Each quarter there will be a 5% decrease in the number of referrals to the child study team. • Every nine weeks, 100% of students receiving Tier 2 and Tier 3 interventions will make accelerated progress relative to grade-level standards as measured by common formative assessments. • Each quarter, 80% of students who began the year below grade level will demonstrate accelerated academic progress, as evidenced by student work and district assessments.

Vetting Your Plan

It is important to vet your strategic plan for its alignment with MTSS. Ask the following questions as you vet your strategic plan. How does the plan:

- Monitor and measure items that are related to meeting the needs of all learners?
- Include direct references to components of MTSS?
- Ensure that the information is easily understood by staff and the community?

You can also vet your strategic plan using a simple checklist. The following is an example of a vetting tool. In terms of your long-range plan, vet it against the following. If you follow this guide, you will have all the necessary components to say "yes" to all indicators. If any are missing, you can go back into the previous planning framework to complete the missing items.

Are the following plan components present?

	Yes	No
Team Information/Stakeholder Engagement		
Vision Statement/Envisioning the Future		
Overview of Key Findings		
Strategic Objectives/Initiatives		
Goals, Benchmarks, and Progress Monitoring		

Does the plan include the following?

	Yes	No
Systemic Use of Data		
Linguistically and Culturally Sustaining Practice		
Tiered System of Instruction and Intervention		

Pause and Reflect

If you have a district strategy, review it through the lens of the previous checklist. Does your plan have all the necessary components for a robust MTSS? What is missing that will be critical to incorporate into future strategic cycles?

Logic Models

A logic model is a bridge in your improvement planning process. It allows you to start the journey from your vision and strategy to the creation of annual action plans. Specifically, it will enable you to define your planned work aligned with your intended results. In our first book, *Universally Designed Leadership* (Novak and Rodriguez, 2016), we discuss the value of a logic model (p. 42):

> The logic model puts the plan out on the table: it draws a direct correlation to what we think will happen and how we will know if it was successful. In the process of defining a district strategy, the logic model forces us to be overt about our work. It makes us be clear about what actions we are taking, how we will measure our success, and what assumptions underlie the work.

The template for the logic model we currently use is adapted from *The Logic Model Development Guide* (W.K. Kellogg Foundation, 2004). We have taken the model and added a planning process step. We have found that without this step, the plans are not likely to succeed. Our expanded model includes a component of planning. We begin our process by considering the vision. How might this manifest in practice? What have our self-assessment process and key findings taught us about the steps aligned best with the antecedents? This work will drive the logic model (see Figure 9.1).

The following is a brief description of each step in the model:

- **Resources and inputs:** What resources are needed to operate the initiative?
- **Foundational planning:** What prerequisite planning is needed to successfully engage in the activities?
- **Activities:** What actions are needed to effect change?
- **Outputs:** How do we demonstrate that the actions have been completed?
- **Outcomes:** How do we measure the results of the actions?
- **Impacts:** What are the greater implications of this work for our systems?

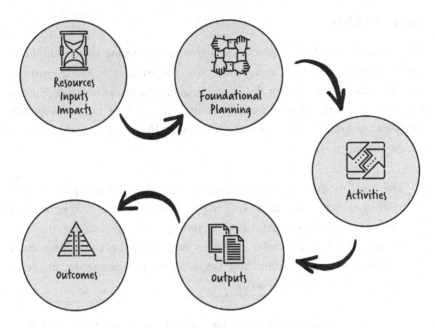

Figure 9.1   Expanded logic model.

Many of our clients and colleagues ask for guidance in choosing the right action steps. If you are looking for a scaffold, you can take the items on the self-assessment that were areas of concern and turn them into action steps. For example, the following is a key finding. We will review the key finding and use the indicators on the self-assessment to drive our action steps, building upon the root cause work outlined in the previous chapter (Table 9.3).

> There is not a common instructional vision understood by all staff, such as through an articulated instructional guide, that details a common set of evidence-based, standards-aligned, universally designed, culturally sustaining, linguistically supportive, and trauma-informed instructional strategies, rooted in deeper learning.

Note how your team can use the self-assessment to inspire concrete action steps to lead you toward your vision. These action steps will be used as a component of your logic model.

Table 9.3 Action Steps for Key Finding.

Categories of Effects (Drawn from the Ratings on the Self-Assessment)	Verified and Validated Root Causes (Drawn from the Data and Document Review, Validated by Staff, and Verified by the MTSS planning team)	Associated Action Steps
Curriculum • Why are there holes in our use of high-quality instructional materials?	There are no district vetted and defined process, protocols, or rubrics used during curriculum adoption that speak to the qualities of HQIM.	• Draft process, protocols, and rubrics to be used during curriculum adoption that speak to the qualities of HQIM.
Pedagogy • Why hasn't the full learning community implemented effective instructional practices (rooted in deeper learning, universally designed, culturally sustaining, linguistically supportive, and trauma-informed) consistently?	There is no definition of instructional practice and no guide to articulate these expectations. In addition, the organization has not identified measures and resources (e.g., observation tools or an instructional guide) to ensure organization-wide fidelity of high-quality instructional practices.	• Draft and share an instructional guide that articulates effective instructional practices. • Identify a common observational tool rooted in these instructional practices to support organization-wide fidelity.

(Continued)

Table 9.3   (Continued)

Categories of Effects (Drawn from the Ratings on the Self-Assessment)	Verified and Validated Root Causes (Drawn from the Data and Document Review, Validated by Staff, and Verified by the MTSS planning team)	Associated Action Steps
Assessment • There is no process for collecting and analyzing student work throughout units to monitor student performance that results in increasing equitable outcomes.	There is no common planning time embedded into the schedule. There are no established protocols for analyzing student work. There has been no PD on effectively using student work to inform instructional design.	• Revise the schedule to include common planning time. • Create a set of common protocols for analyzing student work. • Provide PD on effectively using student work to inform instructional design.

Let's walk through a scenario. Imagine we have found that a large number of students have been referred for special education evaluation who do not qualify, yet many are below grade level in literacy. The root cause process determined that one primary cause was a lack of Tier 2 support. As a result, teachers were overidentifying students for evaluations because no other support structures were in place. The team's vision included this: "We have a universally designed, personalized, flexible, inclusive, tiered instructional model that includes a rich, rigorous, comprehensive, and aligned curriculum measured by authentic assessments." It was time for the logic model to bridge current practice to the vision. Table 9.4 provides a sample logic model focused on increasing student support in literacy for your review.

Table 9.4   Sample logic model.

Related Vision Components: We have a universally designed, personalized, flexible, inclusive, tiered instructional model that includes a rich, rigorous, comprehensive, and aligned curriculum measured by authentic assessments.

Related Initiative: Increase students' literacy scores by creating a more comprehensive approach to tiered instruction.

Related SMART Goal(s): By June, our school will meet our accountability targets, as measured by the statewide accountability report.

Resources and Inputs:
- Purchase universal screening measures to identify students who may be below grade level and diagnostic assessments to understand the specific skills for support.
- Acquire a data management system to keep the data being collected.
- Purchase intervention materials.
- Adjust the schedule to allow for intervention time that would not supplant core instruction.
- Hire and reallocate staff to offer more tiered intervention support.

Foundational Planning Steps:
- Use grant and federal funds to purchase the assessments and intervention materials as well as the data management system.
- Form representative working committees to hire the staff, revise the schedule, select the assessment, and plan the PD.
- Create an assessment schedule and make sure there is the time, staff, and devices needed to proctor the assessments.
- Review the kinds of materials to match the needs of the data and students and to know which interventions were evidence-based.
- Look at the duration and frequency of the interventions to ensure there is enough allotted time in the schedule.
- Locate general fund budget monies to cover the staffing costs and work with union to adjust the schedule.
- Build staff capacity to assess students and use that data to inform evidence-based interventions.

Table 9.4   (Continued)

Action Steps	• Purchase universal screening measures, diagnostic assessments, and intervention materials. • Train staff on how to proctor the assessments and use universal screening measure data. • Redesign the schedule to allow time for collaborative planning and data review and include a WIN (What I Need) block to support intervention. • Hire a literacy coach to support Tier 1 acceleration and Tier 2A support. • Hire two literacy interventionists to support Tier 2 instruction.
Outputs	• Share budget documents and purchase orders to show that the materials and assessments were ordered. • Share the assessment calendar. • Share the evidence ratings of the materials selected. • Provide a copy of the new schedule. • Provide a copy of the position posting and a list of the newly assigned staff.
Outcomes	• Articulate the specific benchmarks for student outcomes on statewide assessments and universal screening measures to define annual growth as a result of their shifted systems. • Professional learning evaluation data is used to define what aspects of PD and coaching worked and what needed to be adapted.
Impact	• Adopt a zero-based budgeting approach. • Expand the model to mathematics. • Institute the new schedule with common planning and WIN across the district.

- **Inputs and resources:** The team decided they needed to use universal screening measures to identify students who may be below grade level and diagnostic assessments to understand the specific skills for support. They needed to adjust the schedule to allow intervention time that would not supplant core instruction. They also recognized the need to hire and reallocate staff to offer more tiered intervention support.

- **Foundational planning:** They realized they needed to do a lot of foundational planning to get this work up and running.

- **Action steps:** Because they knew the root causes, they drafted high-leverage action steps aligned with their findings within their locus of control.

- **Outputs:** They articulated artifacts of practice that would naturally occur once the action steps happened.

- **Outcomes:** They created benchmarks for student outcomes on statewide assessments and universal screening measures to define annual growth as a result of their shifted systems. They designed new observation mechanisms to observe tiered support and looked at the data of practice over time.

- **Impacts:** They realized that the systems needed to change as a result of this work. They began doing zero-based budgeting so that the needs drove the budget and the other way around. The team's original logic model was based on literacy scores, but when they examined math results, they realized that the model would also need to be expanded to mathematics. Because they anticipated that this new schedule would work at the level of these schools, they decided to adopt the new schedule with common planning and WIN (What I Need) at all levels.

Your Turn

Writing a logic model will help you map out all the steps in planning and outline what is necessary and how your team will measure success. You can use the template in Table 9.5 if it is helpful.

Table 9.5　Template for logic model.

Related Vision Components:	
Related Initiative:	
Related SMART Goal(s):	
Inputs and Resources:	
Foundational Planning Steps:	
Strategies/Activities (Action Steps)	
Outputs	
Outcomes	
Impact	

Pause and Reflect

Has your team developed a logic model to drive strategic improvement? If not, consider why your team may have skipped this step. Why it is critical to focus on logic modeling, especially as it relates to differentiating outputs and outcomes to measure your impact on all learners?

Prioritizing Action Steps

Coming up with action steps can be daunting. To support you, we have drafted a bank of sample action steps aligned with essential planning components (see Appendix B).

Although we wish we could do everything in Year 1, systemic planning takes time. It is a helpful exercise for planning teams to prioritize the action steps across the years within the strategic plan. Prioritization may be a result of some steps being foundational to others, or may be prioritized based on need. For example, if a district wants to create a robust data culture, it is important to ensure there are valuable and reliable forms of data before scheduling data meetings. When examining areas of need, if it is found Algebra I results indicate the need to shift to high-quality curriculum, Year 1 would include a curriculum adoption process for mathematics at the high school as well as looking at additional factors like professional development and scheduling. In the example in Table 9.6, the team prioritized action steps over three years.

Table 9.6 Sample annual action steps for MTSS strategy.

Year	Action Steps
Year 1	• Draft and distribute an instructional guide with articulated expectations and resources aligned with UDL, acceleration, and culturally and linguistically responsive practice. (Related lever: instructional design) • Draft a set of articulated prerequisite skills and a corresponding list of high-quality instructional materials (HQIM) curriculum-based formative measures to drive acceleration efforts in Tier 1. (Related lever: instructional design) • Draft an assessment map and purchase assessments, inclusive of universal screening measures and diagnostic assessment to be used in a data flowchart to inform tiered support staffing and scheduling. (Related lever: tiered systems) • Create a scheduling committee tasked with revising the schedule to ensure that all students have access to Tier 1 support via appropriate core learning blocks, access to supplemental tiered support as needed, and flexibility to move across tiers as needed (e.g., through the use of WIN blocks) and inclusive of collaborative planning time for staff to analyze student data to assess effectiveness of instructional strategies and interventions. (Related lever: systems and structures) • Create a PD plan focusing on Acceleration, UDL, linguistically responsive and culturally sustaining practice. (Related lever: systems and structures) • Create a review process and schedule for the purchase of high-quality instructional materials at all three tiers, informed by outcomes data. (Related lever: systems and structures) • Reallocate funding in the staffing portion of the budget to be less dependent on paraeducators and more focused on funding co-taught classrooms, coaches, interventionists, and content-specialists (e.g., licensed reading specialist, ESL instructor), for both English learners and students with disabilities. (Related lever: systems and structures)

(Continued)

Table 9.6   **(Continued)**

Year	Action Steps
Year 2	• Implement a PD plan focusing on acceleration, UDL, linguistically responsive and culturally sustaining practice, inclusive of tiered coaching, related to standards, and the adopted HQIM materials. (Related lever: systems and structures) • Hire instructional coaches and define a set of fidelity measures aligned with the instructional guide that will guide coaches' work. (Related lever: systems and structures) • Implement and staff the new schedule inclusive of core learning blocks, supplemental tiered support, flexibility to move across tiers, and collaborative planning time. (Related lever: systems and structures) • Create a schedule and committee to annually vet assessment maps with a set of criteria aligned with culturally responsive design and accessibility. (Related lever: tiered systems) • Adopt district and school-level data systems to track student performance over time and inform decision-making at all levels. (Related lever: tiered systems) • Conduct a program review to ensure that all multilingual learners have access to appropriate ESL services and are able to access the general curriculum and tiered system of support. (Related lever: tiered systems) • Create a regular vetting protocol to review IEPs to ensure that all SWDs are able to access and make progress within the general curriculum and students are provided tiered support, as appropriate. (Related lever: tiered systems) • Conduct an equity audit of existing policies, practices, and procedures with a focus on issues of disproportionality to inform necessary systems level adjustments. (Related lever: tiered systems)

Table 9.6   (Continued)

Year	Action Steps
Year 3	• Adapt programs based on the reviews of MLL programming and IEPs. (Related lever: tiered systems) • Review the results of the equity audit to make adjustments to the existing policies, practices, and procedures with a focus on issues of disproportionality to inform necessary systems-level adjustments. (Related lever: tiered systems) • Implement a PD plan focusing on acceleration, UDL, linguistically responsive and culturally sustaining practice, inclusive of tiered coaching. (Related lever: systems and structures) • Incorporate the focus on acceleration, UDL, and culturally sustaining practices into learning walks and formal evaluation feedback. (Related lever: systems and structures)

Once you have completed your logic model and organized your action steps by year, you are ready to create your annual action plan inclusive of timelines, persons responsible, and when progress will be reported. We recommend you always consider a primary person responsible from the core MTSS team. That helps guarantee that one person is responsible for ensuring the action takes place. That does not mean they are responsible solely for doing the action; they are in charge of making sure the action occurs and are the point of contact for reporting progress. Table 9.7 provides a sample format to report annual action steps aligned with the district strategy and logic model.

We also recommend creating a template where you can report status updates to all stakeholders. Note how Table 9.8 provides a template for sharing each activity's status and its impact on the related initiatives.

Once you draft your action plan, you can use the review process (Table 9.9) to reflect on its connection to MTSS.

Table 9.7   Sample annual action plan.

SMART Goal: By June, our school will meet our accountability targets, as measured by the statewide accountability report.

Time Frame	Primary Person(s) Responsible	Individual(s) Involved
July–June	Director of Curriculum	• Building principals • Business manager • Curriculum adoption committee • Data specialists • ELA coordinator • HR manager • Union

Defined Output(s)	Defined Outcome(s)	Resources Needed
• Budget documents and purchase orders to show that the materials and assessments were ordered • Assessment calendar • Evidence ratings of the materials selected • Copy of the new schedule • Copy of the position posting and a list of the newly assigned staff	Samples: • 60% of students K–4 will meet grade-level benchmarks in literacy on the End of the Year (EOY) assessment. • We will increase the percentage of engagement within our PD offerings by 10% annually over the next three years.	• Universal screening measures • Data management system • Intervention materials • Updated schedule • Staffing

Table 9.7 (Continued)

Action Steps

- Purchase universal screening measures, diagnostic assessments, and intervention materials.
- Train staff in how to proctor the assessments and use universal screening data.
- Redesign the schedule to allow time for collaborative planning and data review and include a WIN (What I Need) block to support intervention.
- Hire a literacy coach to support Tier 1 acceleration and Tier 2A support.
- Hire two literacy interventionists to support Tier 2 instruction.

Foundational Supports

- Use grant and federal funds to purchase the assessments and intervention materials as well as the data management system.
- Form representative working committees to hire the staff, revise the schedule, select the assessment, and plan the PD.
- Create an assessment schedule and make sure there is the time, staff, and devices needed to proctor the assessments.
- Review the kinds of materials to match the needs of the data and students and to know which interventions were evidence-based.
- Look at the duration and frequency of the interventions to ensure there is enough allotted time in the schedule.
- Locate general fund budget monies to cover the staffing costs and they would need to work with their union to adjust the schedule.
- Build staff capacity.

Summary

Creating a logic model brings together all the work you completed throughout the exploration phase to share your key findings, related action steps, and intended outcomes and outputs. It is not enough to create a logic model and an action plan. As we have shared throughout this book, at every step, you need to share your work with all stakeholders and ask them for their feedback.

Table 9.8   Action plan template with status updates.

Related Initiative						
Increase the literacy scores of students by creating a more comprehensive approach to tiered instruction.						
SMART Goal						
By June, our school will meet our accountability targets, as measured by the statewide accountability report.						
Activity	Time Frame	Primary Person(s) Responsible	Individuals Involved	Q1 Status Update	Q2 Status Update	Q3 Status Update
Purchase universal screening measures, diagnostic assessments, and intervention materials.	July–August					

Table 9.9   **Action plan review template.**

Review Purpose: This protocol can be used to review annual action plans to ensure that they are meeting the needs of all learners and offer authentic opportunities to measure growth.

15 minutes	Presenters share the plan, online or in hard copy, with reviewers for silent text review. Presenters should not introduce the plan and its benchmarks or provide context, but rather allow the plan to stand on its own. After reviewers have had an opportunity to read and reflect on the plan, presenters ask reviewers the following protocol questions. Reviewers provide feedback in as much detail as possible. Presenters listen, ask clarifying questions, and record feedback.
45 minutes	Discuss the following questions. **How does the plan:** • Monitor and measure items that are related to meeting the needs of all learners? • Include direct references to components of MTSS? • Ensure that the information is easily understood by staff and the community? **How do the plan's benchmarks:** • Create clear and specific outcomes? • Identify realistic and achievable time frames? • Support effective monitoring (for example, naming an individual owner and a specific time frame)? **As you review the early evidence of change benchmarks, how does the plan:** • Name the evidence/data source that will be used to evaluate that benchmark? • Explain how you will see that evidence—who will collect it, how, and when? • State how the benchmark is aligned with plan outcomes?

Reflection Questions

1. How does your process of planning a district strategy and annual improvement plans align to the recommendations in this chapter?
2. What are the benefits of engaging in logic models as you create district improvement plans that align to your overall district strategy?
3. What are the challenges associated with logic modeling and how can you address them through proactive and strategic planning?
4. How would regularly reporting status updates in your action plan create transparency and improve communication in your school/district?

10 | Implementing Systems

In this chapter, we focus on monitoring growth and impact as you implement your strategic plan. Given the foundational work you put into the needs assessment and planning process, it is critical to ensure that strategic initiatives lead you toward your instructional vision. Creating robust feedback loops and being transparent about growth will ensure that you will continue to shift your systems to ensure that your district is truly in support of all students. The chapter concludes with a case study of a district that was able to make considerable growth toward its vision as a result of their commitment to MTSS.

Avoiding the Fate of Sisyphus

There is an old adage, "practice makes perfect." We have heard that from countless teachers and coaches, and you know what? They were lying. Neither of us has achieved perfection in anything, regardless of how much we persisted. It is probably more accurate to say that practice makes progress, and we believe that wholeheartedly. But we want to add something to the mix. It's not enough to practice and persist. You also have to monitor progress; otherwise it can feel a little like you're working way too hard and not getting results. And there is nothing more frustrating than that.

As former English/language arts teachers, we are both reminded of the Greek myth of Sisyphus. As the myth goes, Sisyphus ticked off Zeus, and his punishment was to roll a boulder up a hill for all eternity. Regardless of how much he practiced and pushed, that boulder rolled back down. We hear from too many educators and leaders that they feel the same way—they are practicing, pushing, and persisting but aren't making a considerable impact on student outcomes. This is why implementing practices and programs with fidelity and creating a culture that monitors progress is critical. Both of these components are absolutely essential, but too often, the concepts have a negative connotation in schools and districts.

You walk into a meeting of educators and start using the words *fidelity*, *integrity*, and *data-based decision-making*, and you may observe some awkward body language. We know this work is about kids, not numbers, but the evidence is clear. If we want to positively impact the outcomes of all students, there are known practices, programs, and interventions that give educators and students the best chance of success. Using words like *fidelity* and *data* helps to support educators because, let's face it, a lot of the work about what works has been done for us!

When we lean into fidelity and integrity, we provide a recipe for success. The reason we monitor progress is simply that we do not want teachers to push a boulder up a mountain all year to find out after 180 days that they are right back where they started. Punishments from Zeus are no joke, and our educators deserve better.

Unpacking Fidelity

Implementation fidelity is the degree to which a program, practice, or intervention (from herein, we will refer to all as *intervention*) is delivered as intended. Fidelity checks should create open communication and productive feedback by providing educators and leaders with opportunities to learn and collaborate (Dane and Schneider, 1998; Gresham et al., 2000; Sanetti and Kratochwill, 2009). Often, implementation fidelity is used to discuss what happens in classrooms, but in our work implementation fidelity also relates to district and school improvement efforts on a larger scale. First, let's unpack why monitoring implementation fidelity in classrooms is critical.

If implementation fidelity is not consistently monitored, researchers caution that teachers and students are stuck in a black box and may struggle to understand why students aren't making progress. As Smith, Finney, and Fulcher (2017) noted, "Inside this black box could be the intervention as it was designed or intended or an intervention that deviated from what was intended." Leaders can help to paint a picture of intervention fidelity by working with teams of educators to co-create implementation fidelity data. Evaluators and coaches must examine five components of implementation fidelity data on an ongoing basis related to teacher practice (Smith, Finney, and Fulcher, 2017):

- Specific features and components of the program
- Whether each feature or component was actually implemented (i.e., adherence)
- Quality with which features and components of the intervention were implemented
- Perceived student responsiveness during implementation
- Duration of implementation (i.e., the amount of instruction provided, which typically includes the number of sessions and the length of each session)

We love the work of researchers Erica Mason from the University of Missouri and Dr. R. Alex Smith from the University of Southern Mississippi. In their article *Tracking Intervention Dosage to Inform Instructional Decision Making* (Mason and Smith, 2020), they share an anecdote about the importance of monitoring quality and duration:

> Consider how the different causes of the student's unresponsiveness would warrant different instructional responses. If it were determined incorrectly that the intervention was not successful, a teacher might needlessly make significant modifications to the intervention materials, practices, or content or select a different intervention altogether. On the contrary, if it were determined that the student was missing intervention time, a teacher might conference with the student's family or seek the support of colleagues in getting the student to intervention on time and minimize disruptions (p. 94).

Once individual teachers understand implementation fidelity data, leaders can use the data in their own professional learning communities (PLCs) to drive instructional improvement. Note how evaluators and coaches can use the questions that follow as they support educators in implementing evidence-based interventions.

- What are the features and components of the intervention that all teachers need to implement?
- How will we know if they are implementing all features and components with quality?
- How will we respond when teachers are not implementing all features and components with quality?
- How will we collaborate with teachers who use all features and components with fidelity to scale the intervention throughout the school or district?

These examples are focused on classroom-specific implementation, but we also need to monitor the implementation fidelity of our MTSS efforts. When focusing on building a multi-tiered system, there are three basic types of fidelity. These three types of fidelity are generated from the categorized fidelity work in Table 10.1:

Table 10.1 Fidelity categories.

What Is Fidelity?	What Are the Fidelity Categories?
Fidelity is the degree to which the program is implemented as intended by the program developer, including the quality of implementation. • Fidelity = Consistency and Accuracy • Fidelity = Integrity	• **Context:** Necessary structures/systems, and conditions necessary for a program to operate with fidelity • **Consistency:** The extent to which the practitioner uses the interventions and strategies defined by the plan • **Competency:** Level of skill demonstrated by the practitioner in using the core intervention components as prescribed

Source: Adapted from NIRN https://nirn.fpg.unc.edu/module-1/usable-innovations/definitions-fidelity last accessed January 10, 2023.

- **Context:** Fidelity of implementing the critical components of a multi-tiered system of supports (MTSS)
- **Consistency:** Fidelity of using the problem-solving process across all three tiers
- **Competency:** Fidelity of implementing evidence-based instruction and interventions matched to specific need(s)

To determine adherence, we need to select multiple sources of data. For example, to answer the question "How will we know?" we may examine classroom observation data, student outcome data, and staff self-assessment data. Table 10.2 provides examples of each of the fidelity categories and the kinds of products that can help determine fidelity.

We can monitor the fidelity of implementing the critical components of equitable MTSS by continually returning to the needs assessment work, the self-assessment, our logic model, and our action plan. The self-assessment (shared in Chapter 7) was designed to allow teams to look at their readiness

Table 10.2 Fidelity categories and associated artifacts.

CONTEXT Fidelity of implementing the plan	CONSISTENCY Fidelity of using problem-solving processes and structures	COMPETENCY Fidelity of implementing evidence-based instruction
Reviewing Policy and Procedures Procedural review protocols and the fiscal review protocols are designed to help teams regularly review policies, procedures, or practices to assess how well aligned they are to plans.	**Assessing Educator Evaluation** Establish a SMART goal protocol to vet educator evaluation goals so that they are actively working to support student outcomes identified in your plan.	**Using Content-Based Observation Tools** For example, create English/language arts Look-For Guides for observing classroom content and practice.

Table 10.2   (Continued)

CONTEXT	CONSISTENCY	COMPETENCY
Reviewing Systems These are resources that can be used on an annual basis to assess systems related to your plan and are content-specific and systems driven. This may be a literacy system assessment or an equity review.	**Assessing Data-Based Decision-Making** Create a data use self-assessment tool to assess the overall programmatic use of data, or a data dashboard checklist to be used to assess specific data practices.	**Program Review Tools** Adopt features of a structured Foundational Skills Checklist to evaluate classroom/ school/district's approach to foundational reading skills.
Reviewing Materials Create materials to help you review the fidelity of key areas articulated in your action plan. For example, develop a protocol for assessing bias in your instructional materials or use defined databases to assess the effectiveness of existing assessment screening tools for the specific students you serve.	**Assessing Professional Learning** Utilize a UDL PD rubric to assess professional development implementation against the UDL framework.	**Planning Review Tools** Create an instructional planning guide with tools such as a UDL Lesson Plan Review Template to assess individual lessons or a UDL Course Assessment to assess full courses for alignment with UDL.

Table 10.2 (Continued)

CONTEXT	CONSISTENCY	COMPETENCY
Reviewing Turnaround Practices Use level-specific rubrics to assess the implementation of turnaround practices related to your current plan.	**Assessing Student Schedules to Create a Master Schedule** Review tool that includes a series of reflective questions about the master schedule to support leaders in evaluating schedules with an inclusive lens.	**Using Instructionally Based Observation Tools** Use the UDL Look-Fors (Appendix A) or design a set of Inclusive Practice Look-Fors to assess planning materials or conduct classroom observations to give feedback to staff.

for MTSS grounded in deeper learning. Although it is encouraged to use this tool in the exploration stage to inform the planning stage, teams may wish to use it to monitor their progress throughout implementation.

The fidelity of using the problem-solving process across all three tiers requires an ongoing data culture. The following considerations can be helpful as you identify implementation data points to monitor improvement efforts.

- Determine the data needed to monitor and evaluate key aspects of the implementation process, such as communication and feedback loops and professional development activities (outputs).
- Determine data needed to evaluate intervention effectiveness, including performance assessment, fidelity, and the emergence of desired outcomes.
- Determine the data needed by teams, trainers, coaches, practitioners, and any other individuals for decision-making.
- Determine the capacity of the current data system and make additions and improvements.

Fidelity Checks in Practice

Often, schools deliver professional development to staff but then do not have systems in place to follow up on whether all staff are utilizing the practices effectively. It is important to predetermine and regularly apply fidelity checks to ensure that evidence-based practices are integrated and sustain the system of support. Regularly assess that:

- Evidenced-based curriculum and instructional systems exist.
- A valid and reliable assessment system (screening and progress) operates throughout the year and clear data-based decision-making rules are implemented.

Table 10.3 provides a sample throughline of a SMART goal and its fidelity measures: By June, the school will develop a comprehensive assessment map and calendar, define a data tracking system, and use monthly data meetings to support written intervention plans for all students scoring below the 35th percentile on i-Ready, as measured by a completed map, student data, data meeting minutes, and meeting artifacts.

Feedback Loops

Feedback loops are the practices and procedures that monitor your progress to ensure that you're moving toward your vision. Feedback loops are cycles designed to provide school leadership teams with information about implementation barriers and successes so that a more aligned system can be developed to meet the goals outlined in an action plan. Feedback loops aren't just about data. While the data will help measure progress toward student outcomes, it is also critical to have feedback systems to find ways to improve professional development and the organization as a whole.

In many cases, the feedback loops are how you will become aware that some people are resistant to the change and will need additional support and information to feel more secure moving forward. Too often, the measures we use to assess our progress are not construct relevant. Simply, we do not measure what we intend to. If you use the logic model and action planning templates in Chapter 9 and you continue to monitor progress and report status updates, you can avoid this common mistake.

Table 10.3 Excerpt of a sample action plan for SMART goal with identified fidelity steps and measures.

Strategy/Action	Personnel Responsible	Measurement	Inputs/ Resources	Timeline	Fidelity Steps and Measures
Regularly scheduled grade-level data meetings	ELA supervisor, principal	Meeting agenda, notes, and intervention plans that result in increased student outcomes in all literacy measures	Provide professional development on creating a data culture. Schedule time for data meetings.	Monthly	Conduct a periodic review of meeting minutes and intervention plans and review against assessment data.
Create literacy data tracking systems for all students	ELA Supervisor	Completed and updated data tracking systems	Student assessment database. Time for ELA supervisor to enter all available data.	Updated two times a year (BOY and EOY)	Assess the data dashboard against tiered support models to ensure appropriate staffing and scheduling are available to meet student needs.

The purpose of teacher professional development is to increase teacher efficacy and improve teacher practice with the ultimate goal of increasing all learners' outcomes, particularly those historically marginalized. Therefore, true measures of professional development are teachers' increased feelings of efficacy, changes in instructional practice, and increased student outcomes. Too often, however, the quality of professional learning is measured by a simple survey asking teachers if they were engaged and if they would recommend the presenter.

This is not to say that these are not important questions, but they do not provide schools and districts with the data and feedback they need to determine if the PD is doing exactly what it is meant to do. Robust feedback loops, therefore, begin with clear targets and ongoing reflection on progress toward those targets so you can share meaningful status updates with your school community.

This process is outlined in the guidance for the Every Student Succeeds Act. Figure 10.1 presents a visual for feedback loops, shared in a publication from the US Department of Education (2016). The steps in the process for continuous improvement, when taken together, can support better outcomes for students.

As you continue your MTSS journey, be sure to continually review multiple forms of data in a cycle of feedback to enhance program effectiveness and meet/exceed the outcomes of all students. In each cycle, the feedback loop can be likened to the research process, commencing with the formulation of a research question, "Is our action plan effective in increasing the outcomes of all students?" and moving through the iterative phases of data collection, analysis, and reflection. This process is ongoing and is reiterated many times (Venning and Buisman-Pijlman, 2013). To simplify, feedback loops consistently answer the following questions:

- What are our goals?
- Where are we now? (What are your barriers and successes?)
- What do we need to do next to eliminate barriers and optimize success?

Once you determine which sources of feedback you will collect on a regular basis, begin to incorporate feedback loops into your meeting agendas. Having these questions at the beginning and the end of the meeting (or protocol) ensures that the feedback loops are on the agenda.

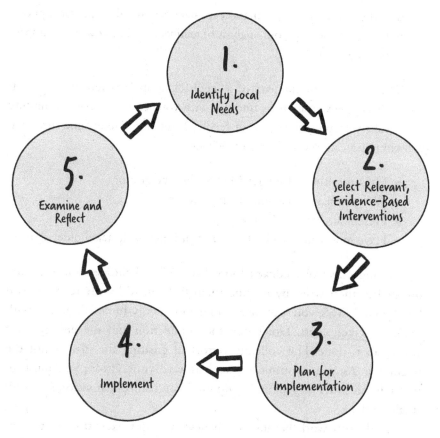

Figure 10.1   Feedback loop cycle.

At the beginning of every planning team meeting, ask:

- Is there any follow-up communication from the previous meeting we have made of others?
- What new sources of feedback do we need to review? (Data meeting minutes? PD surveys?)
- Have any stakeholders requested our input, support, or problem-solving?

At the end of each agenda, ask:

- Is there information we need to communicate to others who have requested our input, support, or problem-solving?

- Is there any more information we need to provide input or support?
- How will we share our analysis of feedback and how will that impact our next steps?

The most important part of a feedback loop is where it often falls short. Sharing any insights or findings with your entire school community is critical to keeping the cycle of feedback moving. Determine how you will communicate the analysis of feedback.

- Meet monthly with your MTSS advisory group?
- Will you have a planning team newsletter?
- Present at each faculty meeting?
- Have representatives on the core team met with stakeholder groups?

Having effective feedback loops keeps all stakeholders engaged and invested in their work by making them feel valued by the team. As you build your MTSS, you will invest time and energy in collaboration with multiple stakeholders. Don't lose the connection and the energy once your plan is done. The collective effort of creating the plan is just the beginning. As you continue to work toward your vision, you must go through this process again and again until you realize that vision for every single student.

We do this work because we believe, without exception, that every single student can learn at high levels and access deeper learning when we get the conditions right. Those conditions require us to change our mindsets, our skill sets, and above all, our systems. We have to commit to changing classroom instruction, our tiered supports, and our systems. This work is possible. We want to end this book with a story of a district we worked with, partnering with them throughout their initial MTSS process. Know that this growth is not only possible but probable if you commit to this journey.

A Case Study: Integrating MTSS

This case examines how a regional district in Massachusetts integrated MTSS by addressing instructional methods, tiered systems, and systems and structures. A core team made up of central office administration, building-based administration, coaches, and teacher leaders began this work in 2016.

The team contracted with us to receive training on inclusive practice and UDL. In addition, the team conducted a book study of our book *Universally Designed Leadership* (Novak and Rodriguez, 2016). Throughout our work, we supported them to complete a document review, data analysis, and root-cause analysis.

In their approach, one key finding was that Tier 1 instruction was not inclusive of all learners in terms of placement, access to instruction, and outcomes. In response, the team created a focused multiyear professional development plan aligned to the goals in the district's strategic plan to increase inclusive opportunities and outcomes for all learners within an equitable MTSS.

Multiple layers of offerings were created to support early adopters and those with previous experience with the implementation of inclusive practices. Scaling the work was also prioritized to consistently increase the baseline and implement a plan for supporting new teachers. Differentiated opportunities were provided for professional development that was designed for all educators (paraprofessionals, specialists, teachers, administrators) based on clearly defined goals. In addition to required professional development, supplemental professional development was flexibly designed based on educator interest, availability, and capacity.

Professional development included keynote presentations on inclusive practices for opening day, full-day workshops, instructional rounds, presentation of information at faculty meetings, book studies, provision of resources to include webinars and written materials, mini-institutes, lab classroom opportunities, and a graduate course series in UDL. All offerings were based on the vision and goals of increasing the inclusivity of instruction to improve student outcomes.

To fund the coaching model, the district prioritized coaching as a high-leverage structure. Decisions were based upon the prioritization of the model. The district aligned the high school and middle school schedules to increase the ability to share staff, resulting in the ability to reduce positions through retirements. In addition to the funds reallocated from these reductions, Tier 1 access for all learners in content areas was prioritized with co-teaching models. This shift to inclusive instruction through co-teaching resulted in a reduction of paraprofessionals. The district did an analysis of all staffing ratios to ensure they were adequate to support rigorous instruction but also foster independence and access to Tier 1. The coaching model in the beginning stages included a full-time coach in K–8 and a part-time coach in K–12 science.

The district used data to allocate these resources, given they were limited in relation to need. Purposeful, data-based feedback loops resulted in making changes midyear to reallocate coaching supports to areas of need. Additionally, two building-based principals who had previously been identified as "teaching principals" were restructured to be coaching principals. As teaching principals, they were focused specifically on providing Tier 2 instruction to a small group of students relative to the overall population. As coaching principals, they were able to impact all learners through coaching in classrooms using coaching cycles with the goal of strengthening Tier 1 instruction to reduce the need for remediation in Tier 2.

Following the first year of implementation, growth was evident in the data where coaching had been implemented. The administration used this data to propose the addition of a full-time instructional coach at the elementary level, and a coaching vice principal of teaching and learning at the middle school level. The district also reallocated staff to create a coaching position at the high school. The science coaching was reassigned to the elementary instructional coach, increasing the time available to the high school. The two coaching principals remained, rounding out the team. The coaching team meets regularly to look at data, engage in professional development, and receive support from the assistant superintendent of teaching and learning.

In 2019, three years into their strategic MTSS plan, all five schools increased their accountability and criterion-referenced score on state assessments. The district's middle school, the only school in the district that was identified as being a "turnaround" school by the Department of Elementary and Secondary Education, exited turnaround status within one year. Specifically, the school increased the percentage of targets met from 8% in 2018 to 77% in 2019.

Take a moment and consider the strategic moves this district made as it built a robust MTSS. Table 10.4 outlines their actions based on the MTSS model for deeper learning.

Table 10.4   MTSS strategic moves of case study district using equitable MTSS practices.

Component	Strategic moves
Tiered Systems: Data-Driven	• A common language for the analysis of data was used to allocate coaching and design professional development. • Teacher teams use a collaborative inquiry protocol districtwide to look at student data and make instructional decisions. • All instructional and curricular decisions were made in alignment with the inclusive practices implementation plan.
Systems and Structures: Staff Development and Competency	• An adult learning culture was established focused on student outcomes in which educators worked collaboratively to improve their practice. • Coaching was specifically aligned to student outcomes and the professional development plan. • A multiyear comprehensive professional development plan was created that prioritized high-quality offerings focused on inclusive practices for all educators. • Professional development was directly tied to student outcomes in what was planned for and continued/discontinued. • A coaching plan was put into place to support a consistent instructional model based on inclusive practices. • Co-teaching was expanded in staffing structures with corresponding coaching and professional development to ensure co-teaching in practice as opposed to only in name was occurring.

Pause and Reflect

1. What do you see as the two to three big decisions leaders made to move MTSS implementation from theory to practice?
2. Is there anything in the team's approach that is similar to something happening in your district?
3. What would you take from the team's approach and bring back to your district team? Why?

Summary

Creating an equitable MTSS rooted in deeper learning is an extensive process that is evidence-based, reflective, and cyclical. Ultimately, the work is grounded in a vision of equity for all learners. For too long, our systems were designed for the mythical average learner and did not embrace learner diversity or variability. Instructional strategies, tiered systems, and structures did not serve many learners, including our students of color, students with disabilities, students from economic disadvantage, and our multilingual learners. Every one of these learners is capable of greatness, but it requires our systems to shift priorities and make the complex changes necessary to shift the outcomes and experiences of our learners. Throughout this text, we have shared a process for better seeing your current system and recognizing what needs to change in order to achieve both equity and inclusion. Now that you have a plan, you must continue this process, continually looping back to determine how your system and structures provide a pathway for every learner to be exactly who they are, and successful in deeper learning experiences that allow them to work toward mastery, identity, and creativity.

Reflection Questions

1. What does it look like to successfully lead an inclusive and equitable school district? What measurements are you using in your district to monitor your progress?
2. As a team, you will determine what systems you have in place to record and track the data metrics you have chosen for district/school

improvement. Where will you record the data and how will you share it? What systems (such as your existing student information system) do you have to house this data? Is it robust enough? If not, what next steps are necessary?

3. As you reflect on your journey in this text, answer the following question: What is equitable MTSS and how does it support all students?

References

Adams, J., and Duncan Grand, D. (2019). New Tech Network: Driving systems change and equity through project-based learning. Palo Alto, CA: Learning Policy Institute.

Aguilar, J., Nayfack, M., and Bush-Mecenas, S. (2017). Exploring Improvement Science in Education: Promoting College Access in Fresno Unified School District. Policy Analysis for California Education, PACE. https://files.eric.ed.gov/fulltext/ED574814.pdf

Alliance for Resource Equity. (n.d.). Ten dimensions: Resource equity diagnostic for districts. https://www.educationresourceequity.org/documents/diagnostic.pdf

American Institutes for Research (AIR). (2018). Strategies for equitable family engagement. https://oese.ed.gov/files/2020/10/equitable_family_engag_508.pdf

Arnaiz-Sánchez, P., de Haro, R., Alcaraz, S., and Mirete Ruiz, A. B. (2020). Schools That Promote the Improvement of Academic Performance and the Success of All Students. *Front. Psychol.* 10:2920.

Bleacher Report. (2010). 1992 dream team: The greatest team ever assembled. https://bleacherreport.com/articles/435593-the-greatest-team-ever-assembled

Bryk, A. S., Sebring, P. B., Allensworth, E., Easton, J. Q., and Luppescu, S. (2010). *Organizing Schools for Improvement: Lessons from Chicago.* University of Chicago Press.

Boudett, K. P., City, E. A., and Murnane, R. J. (Eds.). (2013). Data Wise: A step-by-step guide to using assessment results to improve teaching and learning, Revised and expanded edition. Cambridge, MA: Harvard Education Press.

CASEL. (2019). SEL 3 signature practices playbook: A tool that supports systemic SEL. https://casel.org/casel_sel-3-signature-practices-playbook-v3/

CAST (2018). *Universal design for learning guidelines version 2.2 [graphic organizer].* Wakefield, MA: Author.

California Department of Education. (2021). Definition of MTSS. (2021). https://www.cde.ca.gov/ci/cr/ri/mtsscomprti2.asp

Carnegie Foundation for the Advancement of Teaching. (2019). The Six Core Principles of Improvement. https://www.carnegiefoundation.org/our-ideas/six-core-principles-improvement/

Center for Universal Design. (1997). Principles of universal design. https://projects.ncsu.edu/ncsu/design/cud/about_ud/udprinciplestext.htm

Chardin, M., and Novak, K. (2020). *Equity by design: Delivering on the power and promise of UDL.* Corwin Press.

Choi, J. H., McCart, A. B., Hicks, T. A., and Sailor, W. (2018). An analysis of mediating effects of school leadership on MTSS implementation. *The Journal of Special Education* 53(1), 15–27. https://doi.org/10.1177/0022466918804815

Choi, J. H., McCart, A. B., and Sailor, W. (2020). Reshaping educational systems to realize the promise of inclusive education. *FIRE: Forum for International Research in Education* 6(1), 8–23.

Choudhury, S. (2021). Differentiating between UDL and differentiated instruction. *Novak Educational Consulting.* https://www.novakeducation.com/blog/udl-vs-differentiated-instruction-a-new-perspective

Council of Great City Schools. (2012). Common Core State Standards and Diverse Urban Students: Using Multi-Tiered Systems of Support. https://www.cgcs.org/cms/lib/DC00001581/Centricity/Domain/87/77—Achievement%20Task%20Force—RTI%20White%20Paper-Final.pdf

Crane, K., and Mooney, M. (2005). *Essential tools: Community resource mapping.* Minneapolis, MN: University of Minnesota, Institute on Community Integration, National Center on Secondary Education and Transition.

Curtis, R. E., and City, E. A. (2009). *Strategy in action: How school systems can support powerful learning and teaching.* Harvard Education Press.

Dane, A. V., and Schneider, B. H. (1998). Program integrity in primary and early secondary prevention: Are implementation effects out of control? *Clinical Psychology Review* 18, 23–45.

Dulaney, S. K., Hallam, P. R., and Wall, G. (2013). Superintendent perceptions of multi-tiered systems of support (MTSS): Obstacles and opportunities for school system reform. *AASA Journal of Scholarship and Practice* 10(2), 30–45.

Durisic, M., and Bunijevac, M. (2017). Parental involvement as an important factor for successful education. *Center for Educational Policy Studies Journal* 7(3), 137–153.

Eagle, J. W., Dowd-Eagle, S. E., Snyder, A., and Holtzman, E. G. (2015). Implementing a Multi-Tiered System of Support (MTSS): Collaboration Between School Psychologists and Administrators to Promote Systems-Level Change. *Journal of Educational & Psychological Consultation* 25(2/3), 160–177.

Education Law Clinic of Harvard Law School and the Trauma and Learning Policy Initiative of Massachusetts Advocates for Children. (2019). Students' Voices: Their Perspectives on How Schools Are and Should Be. https://students-speak.org/wp-content/uploads/2020/08/Focus-Group-Report-July_2019-Final.pdf

Ellery, T. (2020). Belonging as a pathway to inclusive: An inquiry into supporting inclusive practice in secondary schools. *Kairaranga* 20(2), 52–60.

Escudero, B. (2019). *How to practice culturally relevant pedagogy*. Teach For America. https://www.teachforamerica.org/stories/how-to-engage-culturally-relevant-pedagogy

Evans, R. (2005). Reframing the achievement gap. *Phi Delta Kappan* 86, 582–589.

Farmer, J., Hauk, S., and Neumann, A. M. (2005). Negotiating Reform: Implementing Process Standards in Culturally Responsive Professional Development. *High School Journal* 88(4), 59–71.

Fixsen, D., Blase, K., Metz, A., and Van Dyke, M. (2013). Statewide implementation of evidence-based programs. *Exceptional Children* 79, 213–230. Doi:10.1177/001440291307900206

Fixsen, D., Naoom, S., Blase, K., Friedman, R., and Wallace, F. (2005). *Implementation research: A synthesis of the literature.* Tampa: University of South Florida, Louis de la Parte Florida Mental Health Institute, National Implementation Research Network.

Gabriel, J. G., and Farmer, P. C. (2009). *How to help your school thrive without breaking the bank.* ASCD.

Graham, P., Kennedy, S., and Lynch, J. (2016). Dare to dialogue: Engaging parents in system change. *Odyssey: New Directions in Deaf Education* 17, 68–71.

Gresham, F. M., MacMillan, D. L., Beebe-Frankenberger, M. E., and Bocian, K. M. (2000). Treatment integrity in learning disabilities intervention research: Do we really know how treatments are implemented? *Learning Disabilities Research and Practice* 15(4), 198–205.

Hall, G. E., Wallace, R. C., and Dossett, W. A. (1973). A developmental conceptualization of the adoption process within educational institutions (Report No. 3006). Austin: University of Texas at Austin.

Hanover Research. (2014). Optimal scheduling for secondary school students. https://www.mansfieldisd.org/uploaded/main/departments/CIA/assets/MasterScheduleStudy/Research-OptimalScheduling_Secondary.pdf

Harlacher, J. E., Sakelaris, T. L., and Kattelman, N. M. (2014). *Practitioner's guide to curriculum-based evaluation in reading.* New York: Springer.

Hartmann, E. (2015). Universal design for learning (UDL) and learners with severe support needs. *International Journal of Whole Schooling* 11(1), 54–67.

Heifetz, R. A., Grashow, A., and Linsky, M. (2009). The practice of adaptive leadership: Tools and tactics for changing your organization and the world. Harvard Business Press.

Hernández, L. E., and Darling-Hammond, L. (2019). Deeper learning networks: Taking student-centered learning and equity to scale. https://files.eric.ed.gov/fulltext/ED603414.pdf

Hirsh, S., Delehant, A., and Sparks, S. (1994). *Keys to successful meetings.* National Staff Development Council.

Hoy, A. W. (2000). Changes in teacher efficacy during the early years of teaching. Paper presented at the annual meeting of the American Educational Research Association, New Orleans, LA. Session 43: 22.

Institute of Education Sciences. (2017). *Introduction to improvement science.* https://ies.ed.gov/ncee/edlabs/regions/west/Blogs/Details/2

International Disability Alliance (IDA). (2021). Universal design for learning and its role in ensuring access to inclusive education for all: A technical paper by the international disability alliance. https://www.

internationaldisabilityalliance.org/sites/default/files/universal_design_for_learning_final_8.09.2021.pdf

Javius, E. (2020). Coaching up at every level: Inside the system of support to improve Tier I. *Leadership* 49(4), 24–27.

Khazan, O. (2018). Are "learning styles" real? *Atlantic.* https://www.theatlantic.com/science/archive/2018/04/the-myth-of-learning-styles/557687

Kraft, M. A., Blazar, D., and Hogan, D. (2018). The effect of teaching coaching on instruction and achievement: A meta-analysis of the causal evidence. *Review of Educational Research* 88(4), 547–588.

Ladson-Billings, G. (1995). Toward a theory of culturally relevant pedagogy. *American Educational Research Journal* 32(3), 465–491.

Learning for Justice. (n.d.). Social justice equity audits. https://www.learningforjustice.org/professional-development/social-justice-equity-audits

Lever, N., Castle, M., Cammack, N., Bohnenkamp, J., Stephan, S., Bernstein, L., Chang, P., Lee, P., and Sharma, R. (2014). *Resource mapping in schools and school districts: A resource guide.* Baltimore, Maryland: Center for School Mental Health.

Lewin, K. (1947). Frontiers in group dynamics: Concept, method and reality in social science; equilibrium and social change. *Human Relations* 1(1): 5–41.

Loucks, S. F., and Hall, G. E. (1979). Implementing innovations in schools: A concerns-based approach. Paper presented at the annual meeting of the American Educational Research Association, San Francisco.

Mace, R. (1998). Designing for the 21st Century: An International Conference on Universal Design. Speech, June 19, 1998, Hofstra University, Hempstead, NY. https://projects.ncsu.edu/ncsu/design/cud/about_us/usronmacespeech.htm

Mason, E. N., and Smith, R. A. (2020). Tracking intervention dosage to inform instructional decision making. *Intervention in School and Clinic* 56(2), 92–98.

Massachusetts Department of Elementary and Secondary Education. (2019). *Guidebook for Inclusive Practice.* https://www.doe.mass.edu/edeval/guidebook/

Massachusetts Department of Elementary and Secondary Education. (2022). *Massachusetts district reviews.* https://www.doe.mass.edu/accountability/district-review/targeted.docx

Massachusetts Department of Elementary and Secondary Education, (2023a). *Center for School and District Partnership (CSDP) coherence guidebook*. https://www.doe.mass.edu/csdp/guidebook/coherence-guidebook.pdf

Massachusetts Department of Elementary and Secondary Education. (2023b). *Deeper learning tasks*. https://www.doe.mass.edu/kaleidoscope/tasks.html

Massachusetts Department of Elementary and Secondary Education, Commonwealth Consulting, and Novak Educational Consulting (2019). Multi-tiered system of support blueprint. https://www.doe.mass.edu/sfss/mtss/blueprint.pdf

Massachusetts Department of Elementary and Secondary Education, Commonwealth Consulting, and Novak Educational Consulting (2022). *Coherence guidebook*. https://www.doe.mass.edu/csdp/guidebook/coherence-guidebook.pdf

McColskey-Leary, C., and Garman-McClaine, B. (2021). Integrating Improvement and Implementation Sciences to Enhance Educational Outcomes. National implementation Research Network, University of North Carolina at Chapel Hill.

McGlynn, K., and Kelly, J. (2017). Using formative assessments to differentiate instruction. *Science Scope* 41(4), 22–25.

Mehta, J., and Fine, S. (2019). *In search of deeper learning: Inside the effort to remake the American high school*. Harvard University Press.

Meyer, A., Rose, D. H., and Gordon, D. (2014). *Universal design for learning: Theory and practice*. Wakefield, MA: CAST Professional Publishing.

Mid-Atantic Equity Consortium (MAEC). (n.d.). An Equity Audit: Is it in your future? https://maec.org/wp-content/uploads/2021/02/Equity-Audit-Considerations-1.pdf

Minnesota Department of Education. (2021). Minnesota Multi-tiered System of Support Roadmap. https://files.eric.ed.gov/fulltext/ED618754.pdf

Nancekivell, S. E., Shah, P., and Gelman, S. A. (2019). Maybe they're born with it, or maybe it's experience: Toward a deeper understanding of the learning style myth. *Journal of Educational Psychology* 112(2), 221–235.

National Center for Learning Disabilities (2021). Research-based approaches to accelerating learning. https://ncld.org/reports-studies/promising-practices-to-accelerate-learning-for-students-with-disabilities-during-covid-19-and-beyond/part-1-research-based-approaches-to-accelerate-learning/

National Center on Time and Learning. (2014). *School resources.* https://www.timeandlearning.org/school-resources/tools

National Equity Project. (2022). Equity messaging guidance for districts. https://www.nationalequityproject.org/resources/tools/equity-messaging-guidance-school-districts

National Implementation Research Network. (n.d.). *Definitions and fidelity.* https://nirn.fpg.unc.edu/module-1/usable-innovations/definitions-fidelity

National School Board Association (NSBA). (n.d.). About us. Equity statement. https://www.nsba.org/About

Noguera, P. (2017) *Taking deeper learning to scale.* Palo Alto, CA: Learning Policy Institute. https://learningpolicyinstitute.org/product/deeper-learning-to-scale-report

Novak, K. (2022). *UDL now! A teacher's guide to applying Universal Design for Learning,* 3rd ed. Wakefield, MA: CAST Professional Publishing.

Novak, K. (2021). If equity is a priority, UDL is a must. *Cult of Pedagogy.* https://www.cultofpedagogy.com/udl-equity/

Novak, K., and Rodriguez, K. (2016). *Universally designed leadership: Applying UDL to systems and schools.* Wakefield, MA: CAST Professional Publishing.

Novak, K., and Woodlock, M. (2021). *UDL playbook for school and district leaders.* Wakefield, MA: CAST Professional Publishing.

Pak, K., Polikoff, M. S., Desimone, L. M., and Saldívar García, E. (2020). The adaptive challenges of curriculum implementation: Insights for educational leaders driving standards-based reform. *AERA Open, 6*(2). https://doi.org/10.1177/2332858420932828

Paris, D. (2012). Culturally Sustaining Pedagogy. Educational Researcher, 41(3), 93–97.

Posey, A., and Novak, K. (2020). *Unlearning: Changing your beliefs and your classroom with UDL.* Wakefield, MA: CAST Professional Publishing.

Rantung, R. C., and Sarmita, R. N. (2020). Business students' perspectives: What makes successful group performance? *International Journal of Evaluation and Research in Education (IJERE)* 9(4), 896.

Rhode Island Department of Education. (n.d.). School Reform Planning Worksheet #2: Theory of Action. https://www.ride.ri.gov/Portals/0/Uploads/Documents/Information-and-Accountability-User-Friendly-Data/Transformation/Theory-Action-One-Pager.pdf

Riley, K. A. (2018). *Place, belonging and school leadership: Researching to make the difference*. Bloomsbury Academy.

Roc, M., Ross, P., and Hernández, L. E. (2019). *International network for public schools: A deeper learning approach to supporting English learners*. Palo Alto, CA: Learning Policy Institute. https://files.eric.ed.gov/fulltext/ED603420.pdf

Rowland C., Feygin, A., Sebastian, F.L., and Gomez, C. (2018). *Beyond accountability: Improving the use of information to support teaching and learning through continuous improvement cycles*. American Institutes for Research. https://files.eric.ed.gov/fulltext/ED592098.pdf

SWIFT Education Center. (2017). SWIFT MTSS starter kit. https://static1. squarespace.com/static/56b90cb101dbae64ff707585/t/5cc1ed15fa0d6 061c22f6a75/1556213016911/MTSS_Starter_Kit_2017.pdf

Saldana, L., and Chamberlain, P. (2012). Supporting implementation: The role of community development teams to build infrastructure. *American Journal of Community Psychology* 50(3–4), 334–346. https://doi.org/10.1007/s10464-012-9503-0

Sanetti, L. M. H., and Kratochwill, T. R. (2009). Analysis of treatment integrity in school-based prevention programming: Contextual considerations and the good behavior game. *PsycEXTRA Dataset*.

Schiller, E., Chow, K., Thayer, S., Nakamura, J., Wilkerson, S. B., and Puma, M. (2020). What tools have states developed or adapted to assess schools' implementation of a multi-tiered system of supports/response to intervention framework? (REL 2020–017). Washington, DC: US Department of Education, Institute of Education Sciences, National Center for Education Evaluation and Regional Assistance, Regional Educational Laboratory, Appalachia.

Scott, L. A. (2018). Barriers with implementing a Universal Design for Learning framework. *Inclusion* 6(4), 274–286.

Smith, K. L. Finney, S. J., and Fulcher, K. H. (2017). Actionable steps for engaging assessment practitioners and faculty in implementation fidelity research. *Research and Practice in Assessment* 12, 71–86.

Smith, O. L., and Robinson, R. (2020). Teacher Perceptions and Implementation of a Content Area Literacy Professional Development Program. *Journal of Educational Research and Practice* 10(1), 55–69.

Thirunarayanan, M. O. (2004). The "significantly worse" phenomenon: A study of student achievement in different content areas by school location. *Education and Urban Society* 36, 467–481.

Thurlow, M. L., Ghere, G., Lazarus, S. S., and Liu, K. K. (2020). *MTSS for all: Including students with the most significant cognitive disabilities.* Minneapolis, MN: University of Minnesota, National Center on Educational Outcomes/TIES Center.

TNTP. (2018). The Opportunity Myth. https://opportunitymyth.tntp.org/

Tomlinson, C. A., Brighton, C., Hertberg, H., Callahan, C. M., Moon, T. R., Brimijoin, K., Conover, L. A., and Reynolds, T. (2003). Differentiating Instruction in Response to Student Readiness, Interest, and Learning Profile in Academically Diverse Classrooms: A Review of Literature. *Journal for the Education of the Gifted* 27(2–3), 119–145. https://doi.org/10.1177/016235320302700203

Turse, K. A., and Albrecht, S. F. (2015). The ABCs of RTI: An introduction to the building blocks of response to intervention. *Preventing School Failure* 59(2), 83–89.

United Nations. (2020). Universal, inclusive education "non-negotiable." UN News. https://news.un.org/en/story/2020/06/1066942

UNICEF. (2013). *The state of the world's children.* https://www.unicef.org/sowc/

US Department of Education. (2016). *Using evidence to strengthen education investments.* https://www2.ed.gov/policy/elsec/leg/essa/guidanceuse-seinvestment.pdf

Venning, J., and Buisman-Pijlman, F. (2013). Integrating assessment matrices in feedback loops to promote research skill development in postgraduate research projects. *Assessment and Evaluation in Higher Education* 38(5), 567–579.

Waitoller, F., and Kozleski, E. (2013). Working in Boundary Practices: Identity Development and Learning in Partnerships for Inclusive Education. *Teaching and Teacher Education* 31: 35–45.

Washington Office of Superintendent of Public Instruction. (2020). Washington's Multi-Tiered System of Supports Framework. https://www.k12.wa.us/sites/default/files/public/cisl/iss/pubdocs/WA%20MTSS%20Framework%20Publication_final.pdf

WIDA. (n.d.). Understanding multilingual learners. https://wida.wisc.edu/teach/learners

W.K. Kellogg Foundation. (2004). Logic model development guide. https://www.naccho.org/uploads/downloadable-resources/Programs/Public-Health-Infrastructure/KelloggLogicModelGuide_161122_162808.pdf

Yoon, K. S., Duncan, T., Lee, S. W.-Y., Scarloss, B., and Shapley, K. (2007). Reviewing the evidence on how teacher professional development affects student achievement (Issues and Answers Report, REL 2007–No. 033). Washington, DC: US Department of Education, Institute of Education Sciences, National Center for Education Evaluation and Regional Assistance, Regional Educational Laboratory Southwest. http://ies.ed.gov/ncee/edlabs

Appendix A: UDL Look-for Tool

This tool can be used by teachers, instructional coaches, and evaluators to observe and set goals for more universally designed learning opportunities in the classroom. The tool was designed with a focus on instructional coaching and instructional coaching questions, because of its documented impact on teacher efficacy.

Table A.1　10 Focus areas for UDL observations.

Provide Multiple Means of Engagement

WHAT	WHY	HOW	How does this impact students?	Instructional Coaching Questions
Learning Objectives Firm grade–level learning objectives, based on the standards, are visible to students and referred to throughout the lesson.	UDL is about firm goals and flexible means. Teachers need to be clear about the purpose of a lesson. The goal must be identified as a method or content standard to plan for flexibility and autonomy in the lesson. Standards posted on the board or a student handout but not discussed exclude students who may struggle to decode them. If the teacher shares the lesson's purpose through a lecture, some students may struggle with auditory processing. Additionally, standards and learning goals that are discussed but not posted require learners to expend cognitive resources remembering why they are engaged in a task or activity. Therefore, it is important that the standards are visible and discussed, so all students know why they are learning.	• Posts lesson objectives • Refers to objectives multiple times throughout the lesson • Clearly aligns instructional materials and assessments to stated goals • Provides opportunities for students to craft their own goals as they work toward those objectives	• Has ongoing opportunities to reflect on where they are in relationship to the goal • Understands the purpose of the lesson and can share in their own words • Crafts personalized goals for how they will work toward the learning objectives	• How are students supported in understanding your goals and creating their own? • How are students supported in connecting the material to their own lives and goals? • What might be the impact if students could see, connect with, and reflect upon goals (both yours and their own)?

Student Identity The learning environment and lesson design affirm the identity of all students.	Neurodivergence is a product of both genetics and sociocultural influences. What students know, how they process new information, and how they process new information is largely influenced by their lived experiences. Identity-affirming classrooms create feelings of safety and trust for students while also honoring their funds of knowledge and models they use to understand the world—models based on their cultural experiences and social relationships. Teachers need to build safe, positive relationships with students and model what they look and sound like to foster collaboration and community and affirm student identities.	• Uses materials that reflect the lived experiences and identities of all learners • With advance notice to students, consistently calls on multiple students, using their preferred names and pronouns, throughout the class session • Warmly interacts with each student in every class session • Helps students build connections with each other	• Positively responds to teacher and classmates • Has a sense of belonging and feels seen, heard, and valued • Feels safe to take strategic risks to become expert learners	• How are students invited into the learning environment and/or learning experiences? • How are students supported in creating a learning community? • How does the learning environment affirm student identity and reflect their authentic selves?

(Continued)

Table A.1 (Continued)

Provide Multiple Means of Engagement

WHAT	WHY	HOW	How does this impact students?	Instructional Coaching Questions
Social Emotional Learning The learning environment and lesson design address the social and emotional needs of all in the classroom.	Feelings of safety and belonging are essential for students to be able to engage with their classmates, teachers and the content. Addressing each student's social and emotional needs is essential for academic engagement.	• Provides options for students to self-regulate their emotional state throughout the lesson • Purposefully plans opportunities and provides structures for students to interact with classmates to collaboratively construct meaning	• Practice self-regulation throughout the lesson • Students interact with the teacher and classmates	• How are students provided opportunities to connect with their classmates? • How are students encouraged to share their social and emotional needs with the teacher and one another?

Table A.1 (Continued)

Provide Multiple Means of Engagement

WHAT	WHY	HOW	How does this impact students?	Instructional Coaching Questions
Collaboration and Community The classroom fosters engagement, collaboration, and community.	All learning is both social and emotional. Research shows that brain networks supporting emotion, learning, and memory are fundamentally intertwined. It is neurologically impossible to think deeply about or remember information without an emotional connection. Brain development is also socially contextualized—we learn through, with, and from our relationships with others. Many learners improve sustained effort and persistence when they have options to collaborate with peers. Collaborating with diverse peers is also a critical life skill.	• Draws out personal and cultural connections of the learners to the content or skill • Uses multiple strategies for students to work with diverse partners (jigsaw, think-pair-share, etc.) • Presents scaffolds to support collaborative work (i.e., sentence stems, group norms, protocols)	• Collaborates productively with diverse partners • Demonstrates agency by using appropriate strategies, tools, and scaffolds to support effective group work	• What opportunities do students have to work with diverse partners in your learning environment? • What scaffolds and tools could you provide to students so they can collaborate more effectively? • How do you respond when you see students hesitant to interact with diverse partners?

(Continued)

Table A.1 (Continued)

The Recognition Networks/Provide Multiple Means of Representation

WHAT	WHY	HOW	How does this impact students?	Instructional Coaching Questions
Flexible Methods The learning design provides students with flexibility in how they learn, make sense of language, and build understanding.	Students have a variety of learning needs and preferences. Their learning profiles are jagged based upon the task, the content, outside circumstances, etc. By providing students with a variety of options to interact with and make meaning of language, content, concepts, and skills, students are more likely to engage in deep learning.	• Provides opportunities for students to customize their learning experience to reflect their learning needs • Anticipates each student's varying needs and provides structures to support each student's understanding (i.e., word banks, sentence stems)	• Customizes their learning experience knowledge and/or understanding of content	• In what ways are students encouraged to customize their learning environment? are students supported in understanding the key vocabulary or symbols necessary for your content? • In what ways are students encouraged to construct their own meaning?

Table A.1 (Continued)

The Recognition Networks/Provide Multiple Means of Representation

WHAT	WHY	HOW	How does this impact students?	Instructional Coaching Questions
Flexible Materials The learning design provides students with flexibility in the scaffolds, strategies, and tools they use as they work toward the learning objectives.	Not all students need the same level of support to work toward mastery of grade-level standards. Too often, teachers provide scaffolds and accommodations to students with disabilities or English language learners but the scaffolds and supports are not available to all learners. UDL practitioners embrace intrapersonal variability and the importance of context in learning. What is necessary for some students may be valuable to other students so it is critical that all students know the tools that are available to them so they can become more expert in their learning.	• Provides linguistic scaffolds to all learners (word banks, sentence stems, and digital tools like voice-to-text) • Models how scaffolds/tools might be used • Provides time for students to reflect on which scaffold(s) would work best to support their learning	• Demonstrate agency by choosing appropriate strategies, tools, and scaffolds to learn and demonstrate and communicate knowledge	• What barriers did you notice in your lesson design that inhibited either student engagement or accessibility to the content? • What were some of the scaffolds you provided to eliminate those barriers? • What would be a good next step for you to continue to remove barriers and offer scaffolds to support student learning?

Provide Multiple Means of Action and Expression

WHAT	WHY	HOW	How does this impact students?	Instructional Coaching Questions
Flexible Assessments Assessments are flexible and construct relevant so students have options for how they share their thoughts, ideas, and skills.	Construct-relevant assessments connect directly to the learning goal, measuring growth or proficiency relative to the target. When we design construct-relevant assessments, there are flexible pathways for all students to show their progress toward firm goals. Too often, one-size-fits-all assessments prevent students from sharing their thoughts and ideas and demonstrating their skills. When teachers highlight firm goals, they can ask, "Is there more than one way for students to share what they know? What can they do?"	• Clearly aligns assessment to learning objectives • Provides clear success criteria and rubrics • Provides exemplars and/or non-examples so students have models • Provides options and choices for assessments	• Demonstrates agency by choosing appropriate pathways to share their learning, aligned to clear success criteria • Proposes alternative assessments for how they share what they know, aligned to objectives and rubrics	• Tell me more about how these pathways allow all students to work toward the same learning objective. • What options do students currently have for sharing their thoughts, ideas, and skills? • In what ways do students have the ability to revise and improve work?

Table A.1 (Continued)

Provide Multiple Means of Action and Expression

WHAT	WHY	HOW	How does this impact students?	Instructional Coaching Questions
Formative Assessments Formative assessment data is used to target instruction and frame feedback.	In inclusive classrooms, it is critical that teachers both universally design and differentiate instruction. Using diagnostic and formative assessments provides in-time feedback that teachers can use to meet the needs of all learners.	• Creates flexible groups of students, based on formative assessment data, to provide targeted feedback and support • Provides students with opportunities to reflect on and revise their work after small group instruction	• Is responsive to teacher and peer feedback • Makes corrections based on teacher/peer feedback • Revises their work and their strategies based on teacher/peer feedback	• How do you use formative assessment data to drive small group instruction? • How do you leverage blended learning models so you can work with small groups of students? • Do students have the opportunity to retake the assessment, based on feedback, to receive a higher score?

(Continued)

Self-Reflection Opportunities are provided for students to self-reflect on their choices and their work.	Learners differ in the ways to stay focused, and self-regulate to stay motivated when learning gets challenging. In order to engage our learners, they need opportunities to think about what strategies are working for them to remain focused, what they are learning and what choices they used to move toward the learning goal. The concept of metacognition is important in all aspects of school and life, as it involves self-reflection about one's current position, future goals, potential actions, strategies, and outcomes.	• Schedules time for students to self-assess and reflect with questions/sentence frames for example, • Did the choice help you learn more about _____? Why or why not? • Moving forward, what choice do you need to advocate for yourself and become an expert learner?	• Practices self-regulation when they are frustrated • Is self-aware and can identify what choices work and do not work for them instead of relying on the teacher • Challenges themselves to become more resourceful and reflective, create new goals for themselves	• What opportunities are offered for students to reflect on the learning and the learning process? • How are those opportunities connected back to the goals of the learning (both yours and theirs)?

Table A.1 (Continued)

Provide Multiple Means of Action and Expression

WHAT	WHY	HOW	How does this impact students?	Instructional Coaching Questions
Feedback Feedback from students, both formally and informally, is encouraged and welcomed.	UDL is about choice and voice. We cannot serve our learners if they do not have opportunities to co-create their learning spaces. In universally designed classrooms, students have numerous opportunities to share feedback about what is working for their learning and how the learning environment could better meet their needs.	• Asks students to propose alternatives to how they learn and share what they know • Asks students to share what is working about the lesson and share ideas for making the lesson more relevant and meaningful	• Takes advantage of opportunities to share meaningful feedback about their learning	• How do you create opportunities for students to provide feedback on the learning process? • How do you acknowledge student feedback?

Appendix B: Sample Action Steps for MTSS Strategy

Coming up with action steps can be daunting. To support you, we have drafted a bank of sample action steps aligned with essential planning components of an inclusive and equitable MTSS.

Vision Action Steps

Components	Sample Action Steps
Shared Vision: The learning community has a shared understanding of high-quality instruction, which promotes deeper learning for all students.	• Draft a vision rooted in deeper learning. • Create a plan for the vision to be present in multiple formats and visible to the community (e.g., on the website, embedded in materials such as handbooks, as part of planning agendas, referenced in budgeting documents).
Grounded in Equity: The instructional vision is grounded in equity, communicates high expectations, and advances equitable outcomes for all learners.	• Vet the vision statement to ensure that it is grounded in equity. If it is not present, update the vision accordingly.

Components	Sample Action Steps
Student Experience: The vision centers around the student experience and creates conditions for student engagement and agency in their own learning.	• Vet the vision statement to ensure that it centers around the student experience.

Instructional Design Sample Action Steps

Curricular Materials

Components	Sample Action Steps
High-Quality Instructional Materials: Materials are bias-free, have empirical evidence of efficacy (high-quality instructional materials/HQIM), engaging content, and are inclusive in design.	• Create a process and form a committee to select high-quality instructional materials.
Coherence: Materials used across all three tiers exhibit a coherent sequence of target skills and knowledge that advances deeper learning (i.e., vertically and horizontally aligned).	• Create a schedule for cross-grade teams to meet to review core instructional materials and supplemental intervention resources.
Vision Alignment: The learning community has a system for reviewing curricular materials and adjusting as needed to align to the instructional vision.	• Create a process and form a committee to assess current instructional materials to ensure high quality, using existing databases like CuRATE or EdReports.

Equitable Practices

Components	Sample Action Steps
Equitable Access: All students receive challenging, grade-appropriate instruction and have equitable access to effective instructional practices.	• Conduct an annual equity audit and use the findings to inform improvement plan action steps.
ESL: All English learners have access to appropriate ESL services as part of their Tier 1 instruction.	• Create a committee to review the evidence base of the instructional materials and approaches used in your ESL programming.
EL Support: English learners, at all proficiency levels, are provided equitable access to grade-level curriculum and have opportunities to develop and practice discipline-specific language.	• Conduct an annual internal audit of services for English learners, to ensure appropriate service hours are present.
SWD/504 Support: Instructional practices outlined in the 504 or IEP and used with students with disabilities must be research-based, provide equitable access to Tier 1 instruction, and be implemented with fidelity.	• Conduct an annual review of inclusion rates to ensure the least restrictive environment is being employed for all students. • Create a committee to review the evidence base of the instructional materials and approaches used in your special education programming.

Pedagogy

Components	Sample Action Steps
Effective Instructional Practices: The learning community implements effective instructional practices (rooted in deeper learning, universally designed, culturally sustaining, linguistically supportive, and trauma-informed).	• Create a multiyear professional learning plan to support the application of effective instructional practices.
Implementation: The organization has identified measures and resources (e.g., observation tools or an instructional guide) to ensure organization-wide fidelity.	• Draft an instructional guidebook inclusive of all aspects of effective instructional practice that will be used in ongoing professional learning and coaching sessions.
High Expectations: There are high expectations for all students across all classrooms, including multilingual learners and students with disabilities, such that students are engaging with grade-level work that advances deeper learning.	• Conduct a biannual internal audit of EL programming and the tiered supports ELs are provided.

Assessment

Components	Sample Action Steps
Data-Informed Practice: Standards-based and universally designed formative and summative assessments are used to monitor student progress toward learning goals and to inform effective instructional support.	• Review common assessments to ensure that they are standards-aligned and universally designed. • Create an articulated resource, timeline, and schedule for data meetings to review the use of curriculum-based formative measures against prerequisite skills to inform classroom acceleration for students below grade level.

Components	Sample Action Steps
Data-Based Decisions: There is a process for collecting and analyzing student work throughout units to monitor student performance that increases equitable outcomes.	• Create or select the annual fidelity measures based on our improvement plan's priority areas.
Engagement: Each student's strengths, progress, and next steps are shared with students and families such that students and families know and can track their progress.	• Design mechanisms for sharing ongoing student progress measures, such as an online student grading portal shared with families.

Learning Environment

Components	Sample Action Steps
Safety: The learning environment is physically and psychologically safe, supportive, and accessible.	• Review and revise our safety plans with a lens toward access for students with disabilities and linguistically appropriate design for multilingual learners.
Belonging: Students experience an inclusive learning environment that recognizes the value of all educators and students.	• Create and administer a student survey and ask questions about their experiences as they relate to how well the organization supports their sense of belonging, agency, and personal value. Use the results to create an action item in the improvement plan.
Feedback: The organization utilizes ongoing feedback cycles from students, families/caregivers, community partners, and educators to build an inclusive, positive school community.	• Create a communication plan regarding improvement efforts that includes defined feedback loops, a schedule for when those feedback mechanisms will be employed, and how feedback will be used in upcoming cycles of inquiry.

Tiered Systems Planning

Tiered Supports

Components	Sample Action Steps
Domains: There is a systemic approach to developing a comprehensive set of tiered supports for all learners across all three domains (academic, social/emotional, and behavioral).	• Conduct a review of tiered programming to ensure it is responsive to all three domains.
Tiered Interventions: The organization creates conditions and systems to provide universal (Tier 1), targeted (Tier 2), and intensive (Tier 3) support to students.	• Draft an MTSS Handbook that summarizes the available tiers, outlines the supports provided across all three tiers, and includes data-based criteria for support.
EL: All English learners receive appropriate ESL services, access to Tier 1 instruction, and can access a tiered system of support, as needed.	• Conduct a biannual internal audit of EL programming and ensure the tiered supports ELs are provided.
SWD: IEPs are designed and implemented to ensure that all SWDs can access scientifically based tiered support as appropriate in the least restrictive environment.	• Conduct a biannual internal audit of special education programming and the tiered supports SWDs are provided.
Engagement in Student Support: Families/Caregivers and students are actively engaged in student support processes/decisions and regularly informed about progress. Families/caregivers receive the information they need to advocate for their children and are informed of their rights to request a special education evaluation at any time during the tiered support process.	• Conduct an annual community survey including specific questions targeted to culturally and linguistically appropriate practice.

Data Systems

Components	Sample Action Steps
Data Systems: All schools have a clear system and process of collecting and distributing universal screening, diagnostic, and progress monitoring to inform placement and progress within their tiered system of support.	• Conduct a formal review of the components of our data systems inclusive of a review of policies, practices, and procedures. • Embed a process for data review to be conducted and articulated in all planning templates.
Assessment Plans: All schools have an assessment plan that defines the purpose, type, and timing of all school-wide and district-wide assessments, inclusive of universal screeners, diagnostic assessments, language development, and progress monitoring tools (across all three domains). The map is reviewed regularly to ensure that it is accessible to all and is culturally and linguistically appropriate.	• Publish an annual assessment map inclusive of universal screeners, diagnostic assessments, language development, and progress monitoring tools (across all three domains). • Vet the assessment map for culturally and linguistically appropriate elements upon adoption of any assessments.
Data-Driven Culture: Leaders and educators create/embrace a culture that centers on the use of triangulated data to assess and address current systems that create barriers for students.	• Survey staff on the data culture in our organization and create action items to address the areas of challenge.
Student Needs: Administrators, teachers, students, and families/caregivers engage in strategic problem-solving processes that identify student needs and determine progress monitoring protocols for short- and long-term goals. This includes students with diverse needs such as those with IEPs and 504 plans and English learners.	• Conduct an annual family/caregiver survey with specific questions focused on assessment information shared. • Conduct a biannual internal audit of special education programming and the tiered supports SWDs are provided. • Administer the SaSS self-reflection tool and use it to create associated action plans.

Access to Resources

Components	Sample Action Steps
Reviews: A regular review of student needs is conducted at least annually to ensure that student needs drive staffing and service structures, as opposed to retrofitting student needs into existing models or assessing positions and/or roles that no longer meet the needs of current students or models that may be contributing to inequity.	• Conduct an internal review of the services students receive across all three tiers. • Review the schedule to ensure flexibility for movement across tiered supports throughout the school year.
Tiered Staffing: The staffing selection, models, and positions are designed to support the implementation of MTSS based on students' needs. Consideration is given to staff titles and duties to foster a positive approach to meeting the needs of all students. Staff is (re)allocated based on student needs annually and during the year.	• Conduct a staffing audit annually with a lens toward staffing positions and ratios aligned with defined tiered support models and chosen tiered programming.
Tiered Scheduling: The schedule articulates when tiered supports will occur, ensures that intervention services are supplemental and not supplanting core instruction, priorities direct student supports in staff schedules, and provides time to administer and review data to identify and monitor students.	• Review the schedules to ensure appropriate time is provided for Tier 2 and 3 supports, based on research and recommendations of program efficacy. • Conduct a review of the schedules to ensure that all Tier 2 and 3 services supplement and not supplant Tier 1 supports. • Review the schedule in alignment with effective instructional practices for appropriate daily core content instructional time. Revise as necessary.

Components	Sample Action Steps
Community Partnerships: Community partners are actively engaged to better support students and families/caregivers and to connect them to social services related to health, social, recreational, and supplemental educational services.	• Conduct the asset-mapping protocol to identify key community resources available within the organization that we can use in the future.
Technology: Educational and assistive technology is available for all students and used in alignment with the instructional vision and to increase access to appropriate tiered supports.	• Tangibly embed MTSS into our capital plans, such as including assistive technology in our technology plan.

Leveraging Systems and Structures

Staff Development and Competency

Components	Sample Action Steps
Professional Learning Plan: The organization has a sustainable professional learning plan that offers coherent, high-quality, universally designed professional development informed by and results in movement toward the instructional vision.	• Create a section in the published professional development plan that speaks to the work's alignment with effective instructional practices.
High-Quality Professional Learning: Educators engage in data-based and relevant ongoing, job-embedded professional learning opportunities including frequent observations and feedback that advance skillful use of high-quality curricular materials and associated educational technology. Professional learning results in effective instructional practices that advance deeper learning and include tiered coaching models.	• Create a budget line, job descriptions, and hire coaches across all three tiers. • Design a coaching manual and coaching schedule that supports the use of data as a means to determine the tiered coaching model.

Components	Sample Action Steps
Collaborative Planning: There is time in the schedule for educators (including interventionists, ESL instructors, and special educators) with designated opportunities to collaborate, analyze data and student work, assess the effectiveness of instruction, plan, and engage in learning experiences that deepen their understanding and implementation of effective instructional practices and provide access to grade-appropriate content for all students.	• Create a schedule that includes collaborative planning time and publish a set of organizational protocols to support the use of data to inform educator practice.
Observation and Feedback: All schools and/or teams have routines and systems for frequent observation and feedback that focus on clearly defined and communicated expectations for effective instructional practices in order to advance deeper learning.	• Create and publish the dates and purposes of feedback mechanisms inclusive of learning walks, walkthroughs, formal evaluation observations, and coaching observations. • Design a schedule of observations and allow for tiered coaching models to occur within the schedule.
Evaluation: There are strategic, unbiased, and transparent systems for evaluation, using student feedback, observation data, and review of artifacts along to make informed decisions about opportunities for educator support and leadership development.	• Review and revise observations look-fors to include overt language referencing effective instructional practices.

Structural Support

Components	Sample Action Steps
Alignment to Vision: Resources are strategically aligned for impact and informed by data, and allocations are vetted with a lens toward access and equity and the alignment between resources and the instructional vision is well articulated.	• Create a vetting protocol to assess the budget for alignment with the vision.
Fiscal Support: The budget provides appropriate levels of funding for high-quality instructional and intervention materials and assessments, key positions, professional development, and so on.	• Create a space in the annual budget narrative to speak to the direct alignment with the vision.
Structural Review: Policies, practices, and procedures are analyzed with an equity lens, such as a review for disproportionality for students of color or accessing the language accessibility of the assessment for ELs.	• Review our capital planning process to ensure it is reviewed with a lens of access and equity.
Technology: There is a clear and consistent process for selecting and evaluating technology products that is aligned to the instructional vision and responsive to student and staff needs.	• Draft protocols and policies for technology product selection and evaluation, consistent with the instructional vision.

Continuous Improvement Cycles

Components	Sample Action Steps
Leadership Commitment: There is an active leadership team that takes responsibility for ensuring that systems meet the needs of all learners. The team has the authority to make resource, scheduling, programmatic, and staffing decisions and has representation from a range of leaders (e.g., academics, student support, special education, and English learner).	• Create a schedule for the improvement planning process to be integrated into existing district and school leadership team meetings on a consistent basis.

Components	Sample Action Steps
Continuous Improvement: The organization engages in ongoing and inclusive long-term (multiyear and annual) and short-term (quarterly and monthly) goal setting and monitoring toward realizing the instructional vision and ensuring each student is making progress, which results in adjustments to the school's structures, programs, and resources (e.g., time, staff, schedules) throughout the year.	• Draft a three-year improvement plan. • Create the annual feedback measures based on the plan's priority areas.
Representation: Voices from all students, families, and communities are used to drive improvement efforts and obtain perception data on the plan's progress. Representation is assessed to ensure participation and engagement represent the community at large, with a specific lens to remove barriers to participation (e.g., transportation or language barriers).	• Include specific questions focused on the improvement plan's priority areas in an annual family/caregiver survey.
Equity Focused: Improvement efforts are grounded in concepts of equity and identify clear goals to close the opportunity gap for all students (including ELs, SWDs, newcomers, SLIFE, ELSWDs, etc.).	• Conduct an annual equity audit and use the findings to inform improvement plan action steps.
Multiyear Planning: A multiyear district strategy process is established and results in a multiyear plan rooted in implementation science. The district plan informs annual district action plans, school improvement plans, and educator goals. Annual action plans include the use of benchmarks to assess progress toward the improvement goals.	• Publish an annual assessment map that is inclusive of quantitative and qualitative measures. • Define the three-year plan's target benchmarks with data drawn from student outcomes data, instructional data, perspectives data, and systems/structures data.

Components	Sample Action Steps
Midcourse Corrections and Continuous Improvement: Based on the data collected through fidelity measures and feedback loops, decisions are made about how to enhance the effectiveness of the work.	• Create and share a set of defined data protocols and data points that will be used by the improvement planning team to guide their work.

Human Resources

Components	Sample Action Steps
Distributive Leadership: The organization has instructional leadership teams or equivalent structures to collaboratively develop and reflect on the effectiveness of professional development, planning, and implementation efforts. Across the organization, team and collaboration structures create shared responsibility and ownership and have an impact on school improvement.	• Set up a representative improvement planning team and schedule inclusive of time to review data and draft goals.
Hiring: Hiring processes and procedures are bias-free and ensure that all candidates have the relevant expertise to meet each student's needs and have a mindset and belief that all students can learn at high levels. The organization systematically reviews staff hiring processes and policies to ensure that they are non-discriminatory, inclusive, and focused on meeting the needs of all learners.	• Review the hiring policies and procedures and determine specific next steps to better diversify the workforce. • Update the hiring manuals to ensure that interview questions reflect our improvement plan's priority areas.

Components	Sample Action Steps
Retention: Hiring and retention policies and procedures include strategies to recruit, mentor, train, and support a diverse educator and administrator workforce that is well-prepared to teach culturally and linguistically diverse students.	• Meet with new hires and design a multiyear induction program to support them, including specific attention to the needs of those who are not yet well represented in the staffing community.

About the Authors

Katie Novak, Ed.D.

Katie Novak, Ed.D., is an internationally renowned education consultant, author, graduate instructor at the University of Pennsylvania, and a former Assistant Superintendent of Schools in Massachusetts. With 20 years of experience in teaching and administration, an earned doctorate in curriculum and teaching, and 12 published books, Dr. Novak designs and presents workshops both nationally and internationally. She is the founder of Novak Educational Consulting, a premier organization for designing and delivering high-quality, evidence-based professional development on Universal Design for Learning (UDL), multi-tiered systems of support (MTSS), evidence-based tiered interventions, inclusive practice, equity in education, and effective leadership practices to organizations worldwide. Dr. Novak's work has impacted educators worldwide as her contributions and collaborations have built upon the foundation for an educational framework that is critical for student success.

Dr. Novak is the author of the best-selling books *UDL Now! A Teacher's Guide to Applying Universal Design for Learning; Innovate Inside the Box*, with

George Couros; *Equity by Design*, with Mirko Chardin; and *UDL and Blended Learning*, with Catlin Tucker.

Dr. Novak's work has been highlighted in many publications, including Edutopia, Cult of Pedagogy, *Language* magazine, *Principal* magazine, *ADDitude* magazine, *Commonwealth* magazine, the Inclusion Lab, Think Inclusive, the Huffington Post, Principal Leadership, District Administrator, ASCD Education Update, and School Administrator. She can be reached at katie@novakeducation.com.

Kristan Rodriguez, Ph.D.

Dr. Kristan Rodriguez is the founder and owner of Commonwealth Consulting Agency, LLC, and has been a professional development provider for over 20 years. Dr. Rodriguez specializes in the application of Universal Design for Learning (UDL) in the field of educational leadership and multi-tiered systems of support (MTSS). Other consulting areas include strategy development, administrator mentoring and coaching, data-based decision-making; tiered literacy, acceleration, IB, and educator evaluation. Prior to becoming a full-time consultant, as a result of her leadership on UDL and co-teaching in her district, students made unprecedented growth. Her work was highlighted in a Massachusetts state case study. Much of this work was outlined in the book she co-wrote with Dr. Novak, *Universally Designed Leadership*, which was ranked in the top 50 books in education on Amazon.

For the majority of her career, Dr. Rodriguez has been serving students and staff in public education, as a classroom teacher, curriculum coordinator, assistant principal, principal, curriculum director, assistant superintendent, and superintendent of schools. She spent her childhood living and learning all over the world. From Europe to Africa to Asia, she attended many prestigious American and international schools across the globe. This experience gave her great insight into the value of global perspectives and the importance of collaboration and community. This work translated into a project that earned her the Ansin Intercultural Research Award from Boston University. Dr. Rodriguez moved to Boston while attending university and lived in the Commonwealth of Massachusetts with her husband for more than 20 years. There she received three college degrees, raised her three sons, and had a successful career in public education. Recently, Dr. Rodriguez and her husband moved to the eastern coast of Puerto Rico to support the island and be close to family.

Dr. Rodriguez spends much of her time developing practical tools and guidance. For example, she authored an "Educator Preparation Partnership Roadmap" (2017) to help diversify our workforce, the *UDL Progression Rubric* (2018) to support evidence-based educator practice, the "Multi-Tiered Systems of Support Blueprint" (2019) to support systemic change, and the "MTSS Toolkit" (2020) to support school and district implementation. Recently, she co-authored *Leadership Implementation Guide for Antiracism and Universal Design for Learning* (2021). She can be reached at kristan@cca-pr.com.

Index

Page numbers followed by *f* and *t* refer to figures and tables, respectively.